DATE DUE

Freedom Through Power

WILLIAM WITHERS

With an Introduction by Adolf A. Berle

The John Day Company
New York

Books by William Withers

FREEDOM THROUGH POWER

THE ECONOMIC CRISIS IN LATIN AMERICA

THE SOCIAL FOUNDATIONS OF EDUCATION
(*with Harold Rugg*)

PUBLIC FINANCE

THE PUBLIC DEBT

THE FINANCING OF ECONOMIC SECURITY

SOCIAL PROBLEMS

THE RETIREMENT OF THE NATIONAL DEBT

Contents

Introduction

Power is a vast subject; no important analysis of it has appeared since 1938 when Bertrand Russell published *Power, A New Social Analysis*. Worse yet: power in America is a semantically "dirty word," suggesting inherently noxious phenomena, to be reduced, combated, attacked by sound thinkers, liberal or conservative, or idealized by extremists, Fascist or Communist. The notion that power is an essential ingredient of society—indeed that it is a necessary instrument in providing freedom—will come as a shock to some. Embattled conservatives believe firmly in private property and "individual initiative"; they know—and are right in knowing—that power can prevent them from doing as they wish with their own. It well may prevent any or all of them from owning as much as they would like to do. Practicing liberals as a rule consider power as an obstacle to free development of individuality; they do not like it, wherever and whenever encountered. Left-wing extremists, accepting the principles of Communism, are not repelled by power but in their circles "freedom" has become a "dirty word." They know, and are right in knowing, that any conception of freedom may well prevent them from doing what they want with the dictatorial or semi-dictatorial paternalist power they intend to attain and use in wiping out capitalist civilization.

Below these political attitudes lies a fundamental proposition which I here state without elaboration. Power, fragmented and reduced to possession, tends to become, and ultimately does become, property. Property, aggregated and necessarily managed by an organization, generates, and tends to become, power. By consequence, power and property are not different from each other. Ultimately they are the same phenomenon in different phase of organization. That proposition, only recently studied, is bound to revolutionize both economic and political thought.

Economics, under the mixed statist and corporate organization we have today, and described in this volume by Professor Withers, under compulsion of technology, population pressure and demand, is highly organized and concentrated. Modern economic structure thus polarizes around power centers, at least in major fields of production and distribution. Individually owned "property" (preponderantly stock in or claims against corporations, and homes and automobiles used for consumption) becomes increasingly an economic device permitting the holder to consume more or less as he chooses, but not much else. Power, gravitating to corporation managements and the state, dominates the production of goods and services. The revolutions of our time, nominally fought against injustice to man imposed by property, thus produced less essential change than was conceived by their authors. By almost abolishing private property, Communist civilizations leapt into a civilization of power—as indeed they intended to do; that is, they jumped from one end of the spectrum to the other but did not change its real content. This is why the Soviet Communist commissar of today is own brother to the American corporate executive, except that—being a government and not a private bureaucrat—he enforces his decisions by state police and prison sentences, whereas the American corporate manager and his close cousin, the labor union executive, enforces them by imposing the penalty of unemployment.

If, therefore, individualist freedom and democracy are to be preserved, we have to deal with a number of factors new in social and economic history.

Thus far we have discovered no means of producing sufficient to maintain the standard of living desired without great and concentrated economic organization. This is a result of technology whose productivity, as Professor Withers points out, is organized by a superstructure of institutions. Their power to exact conformity and obedience is great enough to leave the individual nowhere, unless it works against and in a context of counterforce, grounded in beliefs and philosophy, capable of defining goals from time to time and of making itself effective by viable institutions and systems of control.

I disagree with Professor Withers' acceptance of the reality of a "power élite," and because I disagree, especially commend his discussion of it. Unless, of course, a "power élite" is defined merely as a statistical group comprising all the men and women having the training, capacity or environmental experience enabling them to assume high positions in the current structures of national organization. Such a group might be described as an "élite" (if you like the word— I do not). But as a group it has no power whatever. No member of it has power because he is included. Each has to conquer or gain through extraneous institutional processes whatever power he may have. And when attained, it is individual to each, arising not from the supposed "élite" group but from the institution he may have created or come to administer.

"Freedom" perhaps can best be defined as the capacity of each individual to achieve and the determination of the state to protect him in exercising that degree of power essential to permit him, so far as possible, to make his own life instead of having someone else make it for him; this, as Professor

Withers accurately observes, includes freedom within an enterprise as well as freedom outside his job; freedom of life within the framework of government, as well as freedom to go beyond it; freedom of life within large organizations as well as freedom to live outside them.

This handful of words adequately suggests the necessity of rethinking great areas both of governmental and economic theory. No longer is it possible simply to take power away from leaders in power concentrates (Withers' phrase) such as private corporations. The concentrates are there, not by accident, but because they are efficient. Rather the task will be that of setting up countervailing power centers—among which agencies of the federal government will certainly be important elements.

Planning, of the style so brilliantly developed in France by my friend Pierre Massé, will be one of the requisite lines of development. Power can no longer be got rid of simply by not having it. Not in the twentieth century. One can not even be "free" without it: the economic results of its cessation would be oppressive and might be disastrous. Starvation and anarchy outrank even brutal dictators as destroyers of freedom, however freedom may be defined. Freedom thus involves understanding power, learning how to use it and how to check it; and checks will arise in part by means of institutionalized counter-power.

More will be required, nevertheless, than merely opposing federal power to the power of private corporations, or labor-union power to financial power, though both play their part; more, indeed, than opposing national planning power to the blind, oppressive forces let loose by supposedly free markets. Freedom will require institutional protection of individuals in those areas in which individuals can and should make decisions.

In modern life the idea and protection of private property was gradually erected as a defense against dictatorial, feudal and, later, royalist power. Men could not be free if enjoyment of their homes and their daily bread were dependent on the grant, grace and acquiescence of a baron, duke or king. The institution of private property was abused. In the twentieth century, Communist revolutions sought to end oppressive abuses of great accumulations of property—really because they had generated a new power structure. By the irony of history, these revolutions tossed men back into a power complex in which, once more, they could live only by grant, grace or mandate of party bosses or committees—whose own lives in turn depended on a central government, usually operated by dictator named Stalin, Tito, Castro or Mao Tse-tung.

America escaped the revolutionary process. She finds herself now in a civilization depending on power but also insisting on individual freedom. Protections accorded to property as a means of freedom in the days of the eighteenth- and nineteenth-century revolution now must be readapted in terms of providing norms for aid protecting the decision-making power of individuals. These appear to be the terms of reference provided us by the latter half of the twentieth century.

Thinking all this through, and elaborating ways and means of meeting the problem, is a man-size job. What Professor Withers is here proposing is nothing less than beginning the twentieth-century revolution—releasing us from the combined semantic and psychological enslavement (pro or con) to the revolution proposed by Karl Marx in 1848 and distorted half a century ago into what is now called "Leninism." Students of political science as well as plain individuals will find Professor Withers' ideas as clear as they are refreshing.

ADOLF A. BERLE

Columbia University
New York
June, 1965

Foreword

Sɪɴᴄᴇ the depression of 1929 and the early days of the New Deal, no essentially new movement, either liberal or conservative, has developed in American political life. The years since 1937, especially since the Truman Administration, have been politically uncreative and sterile. Liberals have added little to the structure built by Franklin D. Roosevelt and his advisers. Conservatives like Dewey and Eisenhower have accepted a large part of this structure; those like Goldwater have turned farther to the right than Landon and Hoover. Moreover, it can hardly be said that the anti-communist politics of McCarthy and Nixon and the civil rights efforts of liberals on behalf of Negroes have amounted to anything really new in American politics, apart from the extremity to which these movements have gone.

In fact, the terms liberalism and conservatism, unless identified with socialism or reactionism, have lost meaning in the United States. Conservatives talk of basic principles which must be revived, but when these principles are interpreted to mean a return to the kind of government we had before New Deal days, the majority of conservatives will have none of it. Liberals, on the other hand, reject not only communism but any appreciable movement in the direction of socialism as well. The nonreactionary elements in both the Democratic and the Republican parties have not been very far apart on domestic policies, and have agreed completely on foreign policy.

But political and economic progress in our country requires a revival of ideological differences if for no other reason than to promote greater clarity. There are underlying differences of interest and belief which are of great significance, and which can never result in clear- cut issues so long as they are vaguely expressed and hidden by a hard overlying crust of both liberal and conservative clichés. We need to ask ourselves: What is the real difference today between a liberal and a conservative? Surely the difference does not consist merely of leftist and rightist New Dealism.

It is the thesis of this book that liberalism is basically the defense of individualism viewed broadly as the fullest opportunity for personal development. As such, it has been and is now a struggle for the freedom of the individual against the domination caused by the concentration of power. If this were realized, new meaning would enter into our political life and more serious issues might divide our two major parties. One party, at least, might return to the defense of the average man, who lacks both freedom and power, except insofar as he can obtain them through political action. The small man in the United States is again becoming the forgotten man. Having acquired a measure of social security through the New Deal and the prosperity after World War II, he needs to regain a modicum of freedom in our increasingly power-structured society. He needs a New Deal which fights the power groups for him. How this can come about is a broad and complicated question. But its answer certainly requires a reexamination of the nature of power in the United States. This book is devoted to an analysis of the power problem, and the struggle for freedom first against, and then through, power. It ends with an attempt to find new means of restoring freedom and power to the small man.

I

Democracy and Individualism

AMERICANS suffer from the myth that they provided the cradle for democracy, and that having given it birth, they alone are sending it forth to save the world from the sins of autocracy, fascism, and communism. This heroic attitude first appeared in World War I, which, according to Woodrow Wilson, we fought to "make the world safe for democracy." After an interim of twenty years during which we were preoccupied first with great prosperity and then with deep depression, we resumed our heroic posture in World War II in the fight against Nazism. Subsequently, under Truman and Eisenhower, we fought a cold and occasionally hot war against communist totalitarianism. Under Kennedy our democratic leadership became even more pronounced and dramatic.

But in adopting this heroic attitude that we are the protectors of democracy, we have made several dubious assumptions. We have assumed that Americans are wholly dedicated to the principles that gave them birth and that they fully understand these principles in the context of a constantly and vastly changing industrial society. In view of our attempt since World War II to lead the democratic world, it is important at this stage of history to contemplate seriously a number of basic questions. Just how dedicated are we to the principles of democracy? How democratic were we when we

1

set forth to save the world for democracy under Wilson? How democratic were we when, under Roosevelt, we backed England against Hitler? How democratic are we now in our struggle against communism?

AMERICAN DEMOCRATIC LEADERSHIP

In the years since World War II our leadership of the so-called free world has not been wholly effective. To be sure, we have been successful in promoting the economic rehabilitation of the noncommunist nations through the Marshall Plan, and we have succeeded also in organizing NATO and establishing a world peace organization on our own soil. We have created SEATO, an Asian NATO, and have contained communism by impeding its advance beyond certain fairly well-defined boundaries. In Latin America we developed the Alliance for Progress and succeeded in getting the Organization of American States to line up against communist Cuba. But what we have accomplished is more in the nature of democratic defense than constructive offense. Certainly the parts of the world we have defended have become no more democratic than they were before we defended them, and what democracy exists within their borders can hardly be attributed to American efforts except that it would not have existed had we permitted wholesale fascist or communist aggression. When the firing ceased after World War II, we permitted what little democracy there was in China, North Korea, East Germany, Poland, Czechoslovakia, Hungary, Rumania, and Bulgaria to be wiped out, and we have done little to restore democracy either in these nations or in Spain and Yugoslavia.

Americans have not been able to do much more than defend democracy against aggression. They have *advanced* democracy very little because they have not been able to "sell" the American way to other peoples by arousing any marked enthusiasm for it. And the reasons are not hard to find. To use a simple analogy, one may cite a fictitious and ambivalent vacuum cleaner salesman. As he goes from door to door, he is not making sales. This can be explained in a number of ways. He may not understand the company's product and its merits, or he may understand them only superficially. He cannot answer questions successfully or counter the objections of customers. Or it may be that he knows the product thoroughly, but is convinced that it would be better to sweep the floor with a broom or with a competitor's vacuum cleaner. Or perhaps his prospective buyers already have vacuum cleaners which he suspects are better than his. The weakness of American democratic leadership in the world is due to a similar ambivalence concerning the merits of democracy, arising largely from a lack of understanding of its present-day nature. How can we, a people with so rich a democratic heritage, have arrived at such a position of uncertainty?

THE ESSENCE OF DEMOCRACY AS INDIVIDUALISM

The essence of democracy lies in the rights and potentialities of the individual. Any elaboration of democratic doctrine which goes so far beyond the individual as to lose him as the central object of democratic purpose departs from the very basis of democracy. Majority rule or constitutional government are democratic only insofar as they promote the free growth and development of the individual. Rights, liberty, and equality are not valuable *per se* but because they are the means to one fundamental end, individual development. A number of phrases used by Harold Laski aptly express this point of view. He says that a free state seeks to "release individuality," [1] and "prevent the frustration of the creative impulse." It leaves room for "our personal initiative," [2] and provides opportunities "shown to be essential to the develop-

1 Laski, Harold J., *Grammar of Politics*, p. 142
2 *Ibid.*, p. 143

ment of personality." [1] Democracy, according to Laski, is the "affirmation of one's essence." [2] Similar phrases might be quoted from the writings of John Dewey, whose general approach to democracy was in terms of the free development and growth of the individual.[3] Failure to accept the view that democracy is a form of individualism is the cause of much of our ambivalence about it.

INDIVIDUALISM OR MATERIALISM?

Granted that democracy is basically concerned with individualism, the treatment of democracy by Americans since colonial days raises two questions: (1) Did Americans really want democracy defined as the development of individual potentiality? (2) Did they live in such a way as to promote individual growth in this psychological sense? In other words, did the social structure which evolved in this country in the latter half of the nineteenth and the first half of the twentieth centuries promote this type of democracy?

Regarding the first question, it may be said that Americans present a peculiar paradox. Although accepting individualistic traditions and self-interest creeds, they have always been among the least individualistic of peoples. Our social life is full of examples of desire for likeness rather than difference. Our desire for conformity seems to have been evident even in early Puritan life. The dissenters from the Anglican Church established an incredible body of regulations which profoundly restricted the behavior of individuals. Nothing could have been farther from their intent than the promotion of individual development—except within the rigid patterns prescribed by their sectarian versions of the Protestant ethic. In short, they were nonconformist so far as the religion of the Anglican Church was concerned, but highly

1 *Ibid.*, p. 144
2 *Encyclopaedia of the Social Sciences*
3 *Cf.* Dewey, John, *Democracy and Education*

conformist within the confines of their own chosen sects. If we examine American life from its earliest days to the present, how much of it reveals that our major objective was really the growth of the individual as such? Most of our early religious training was an attempt to understand the Bible as God's *unquestioned* word. Much of our early elementary and secondary schooling was rote learning. Not until John Dewey and Colonel Parker introduced elements of individualism into educational philosophy and methodology in the twentieth century did educators begin to concentrate upon this aspect of education. The psychology that lay behind American teaching in these earlier years was essentially mechanistic, concerning itself little with personality.

When we arrived on the shores of North America, one thing was evident: a shortage of means to satisfy material wants. For years we worked vigorously to meet our material needs by clearing forests, growing crops, saving money, creating productive capital investments, exploiting natural resources, removing the menace of hostile Indians, building countless homes and factories, extending vast transportation lines from coast to coast, and ultimately building ourselves into the wealthiest and most productive nation, economically, in the world. In all of this, was our goal the freedom and psychological development of the individual, or was it rather the satisfying of our material needs through a rigorous, free, individualistic form of action which proved more effective as a method of material progress than governmental ownership or control?

If we look back over our more recent history, it is evident that we have not lived in ways that ultimately promoted freedom. After the Civil War came the growth of large-scale manufacturing and monopoly. Large-scale manufacturing brought the factory system, which caused a serious loss of individual freedom in that it took away the ownership of the means of production from the persons who used these means and who were basically dependent upon them for their livelihood. But more than that, it "organized" men in their work lives. Any factory system, to be efficient, must follow planned routines, with numerous workers specializing in limited tasks repeated on the basis of preplanned orders. The life of the factory is one of planned individual regimentation. Individualism in day-to-day activity is considerably limited and circumscribed.

A good deal of our early individualism centered on the market and found its expression in rigorous competition. Business men sought to outdo each other in lowering prices, bringing out new products, improving quality, and generally seeking to win over customers and defeat competitors. One can imagine our early economic life as a struggle for individual survival that fitted the ideal of Herbert Spencer—a survival of the fittest. And no one can deny that in some phases of American economic life a bitter struggle continues. But there has been a great decline in price competition, and the philosophy of "live and let live" has largely superseded that of "dog eat dog." Market conditions range from pure competition to monopolistic competition, oligopoly, duopoly, and, in some cases, almost pure monopoly.[1] But in the major centers of economic activity prices and output are more controlled and administered than not. The individual has little freedom or initiative here except insofar as he becomes a powerful corporate executive or labor leader who because of his power individually plays an important role in the determination of prices or wages.

To expand the picture, consider the role of the owner of property. If he is a home owner, he is circumscribed by numerous regulations and restraints that would have seemed

[1] By monopoly, we mean control of prices or a market by one business; by duopoly, control by two large firms; by oligopoly, control by a few large firms; and by monopolistic competition, partial control by a dozen or more firms.

strange indeed to his frontier or agrarian ancestors. The same can be said of the person who owns a store or a small farm. If one's ownership is in the form of intangible property such as stocks and bonds, the situation is one of absentee ownership where control is limited to stockholders' meetings and other indirect processes. The average shareholder today has little control over his property if he owns stock in a large corporation. Theoretically, he has vast power and could exercise great initiative, but the highly complicated and organized nature of the modern large corporation usually relegates the stockholder to the role of critic or passive acceptor of things done by a few executives.

Finally, the imperative need to sell greater and greater masses of goods produced by large-scale American enterprise has made it necessary (or made it seem necessary) to control the consumer through extensive advertising and other sales efforts so that he will buy the requisite amounts and buy them in time to fit in with planned production schedules. To do this means that the consumer must lose his individuality and be captured by certain uniformities of thought related to mass production. If, for example, one million cars, all alike, must be sold, there must be one million buyers who have been "educated" to feel that they would be happy with these cars, all of them alike. Within this one million buyers, at least, there is very little room for individual difference. To be happy with these cars rather than with others means that there must be a considerable amount of mental regimentation as to behavior patterns and goals. Only a little thought about the thousands of advertising appeals will lead anyone to conclude that for the most part the American consumer is being made to want considerable uniformity. Because of mass production there *must* be uniformity. The product cannot be patterned to numerous individual differences and remain a mass-produced article. As a result, countless individuals must be molded into a uniform mass to conform in their desires and goals to the mass assembly line.

We return therefore to our original question. Did Americans ever really want to be individuals or did they merely want to escape from religious restraints? If the latter is not true, why did they persist after the middle of the nineteenth century in developing a social life that increasingly and in some cases overwhelmingly reduced individualism? Or were they caught unknowingly in a trap, so that before they knew it they were irretrievably involved in the web of conformity spun by the factory, the machine, the corporation, and modern advertising? Hardly! It is more likely that from the beginning, Americans were more wedded to materialism than to individualism, and that where they had a choice, or could make conscious decisions, they chose the solution that led to greater material satisfaction, even at the sacrifice of individual freedom. And it is a choice that many of the peoples of the world, less materially fortunate than we, are now making.

REASON AND CONSENT

If the individual is to do what he thinks best, unhampered by the restraint of other individuals and of society, he must not be bound by rules and restraints *superimposed upon him*. No one has ever contended that liberty is license or that individual psychological development occurs best in the absence of all restraint. What is asserted is that *we must make our own restraints through understanding their necessity for our welfare and that of others*. If these restraints are imposed upon us by others, as they inevitably will be, it must be with our consent. We must understand and approve of them and have some part in their making. In the eighteenth century, these man-made accepted restraints of "public laws" were thought to approximate in many instances God-made, or natural, laws which could be understood and accepted through study. And apart from the scholars, the study of the Bible by ordinary men was motivated to some extent by a sincere desire to *understand* God's law and accept it rationally.

Many of these early democratic beliefs derive from John Locke, who opposed the view that monarchs or princes made law and were above it and the individual was subject to divine right. In opposition, he postulated a body of natural law to which monarchs were subject and which God had created. Monarchs had to accept natural law and the human rights imbedded in it. They did not make the law. Lawmaking was a process of accepting natural law in which the people could participate with the monarch; it was based on reason. It consisted, as Jefferson said, of accepting "self-evident truths." Therefore, it rested firmly on the consent of the people.

All-important here are reason and consent. After Locke, both the existence of natural law and the ability to discover it and appeal to it were questioned by David Hume and others. And rather than persist in the uncertainties of a situation in which human rights depended upon such an appeal, men like Jeremy Bentham and James Mill flatly based human rights on the pursuit of happiness and on the usefulness of law or democratic decisions for the achievement of this end. With the advent of the utilitarianism of Bentham and Mill in the early nineteenth century, democracy came to mean reasonable individual action directed by the majority of individuals for their happiness, the greatest good to the greatest number.

Reduced to simple terms, the democratic citizen wanted freedom to decide on a reasonable basis what was best for his happiness and to consent to rules and restraints only if he could see why they were necessary for this happiness. And since everyone could not have regulations of individual action always to his liking, regulation would have to be tolerated if based on majority vote. But it was not to be blind acceptance of majority rule. The majority had to appeal to reason and explain its action. In addition, even the majority could not transcend certain rights which were freed from legislative action and protected by the courts as inalienable, such as freedom of speech and of religious worship. Thus the democracy of Locke, the basis of American democracy, was one of *limited* popular sovereignty, as is attested by our federal and state bills of rights.

It is this necessity of explanation and consent that Americans may never really have accepted. There has been a considerable reduction in our ability as individuals to consent to anything and in our right to an explanation. More and more things are done for us, because of our ignorance or apathy. It is the leader who understands and decides, rather than a majority of individuals. We may decide upon our leaders, and even here our choice is often limited, but once having chosen leaders, we transfer vast power to them.[1]

Whether we ever really accepted democratic individualism is questionable. That American society changed so that it was hard to make it fit is unquestionable. This is due largely to the changes which occurred in economic and social life in the nineteenth century. Woodrow Wilson was the earliest of our Presidents to fully realize this fact and to be deeply concerned about it. He said: "We have changed our economic conditions, absolutely, from top to bottom; and with our economic society, the organization of our life. The political formulas do not fit the present problems; they read like documents out of a forgotten age.... The new order of society has not been made to fit and provide the convenience and prosperity of the *average man* [italics mine]." [2]

[1] Cf. Myrdal, G., *The American Dilemma*
[2] Wilson, Woodrow, *The New Freedom*, pp. 3-4

THE IMPORTANCE OF THE AVERAGE MAN

Most democratic thinking concludes that the consent and independent action of the individual or average man are of great importance. The faith that Jefferson had in an agrarian society as the bulwark of democracy was largely a faith in the individual who could assert himself if he enjoyed the economic independence of the small farm and was not obliged to knuckle under to such urban power groups as large banks or corporations. Much of the fear of the banks in Andrew Jackson's day was a fear of the subordination of the average man to an aggregation of economic power. This same concern is to be found among the progressives of the early twentieth century. Let us again listen to Woodrow Wilson: "In most parts of our country men work, not for themselves, not as partners in the old way in which they used to work, but generally as employees—in a higher or lower grade—of great corporations. There was a time when corporations played a very minor part in our business affairs, but now they play the chief parts, and most men are servants of corporations." [1] But this was not a tragedy to Wilson, except in that it subordinated the individual. "If the corporation is doing the things that it ought not to do, you really have no voice in the matter and must obey their orders—your individuality is swallowed up in the individuality and purpose of a great organization." [2] And he continues, ". . . the everyday relationships of men are largely with great impersonal concerns, with organizations, not with other individual men." [3]

These are concerns of consent and understanding. But what of the more fundamental problems of originality or of frustrated individual development? In some ways it is

[1] Wilson, op. cit., p. 5
[2] Ibid., p. 6
[3] Ibid., p. 7

more important that human potentials not be wasted than that we have a government of consent. The early believers in democracy were believers in the goodness of the individual man. If he were educated in the rules of right reason, he could make great progress. His mind was a kind of *tabula rasa* on which reason could write. Once having written, it could greatly expand the social achievements of men and the bounds of knowledge itself. In politics, the educated man, or at least the majority of such men, could arrive at the wisest decisions. These were not merely decisions leading to the greatest good for the greatest number, but decisions leading to a more abstract general rightness called the general interest or the general welfare. The faith in the average man and in the education which would develop his potential was enormous. This faith, as we have suggested, was twofold. It was a faith in man's ability through development to improve himself and society, and a faith in his ability to arrive at reasonable political decisions which would be better for the general interest or welfare than those of any one individual, no matter how wise and benevolent.

The average men, Wilson believed, were to be found mainly in the growing middle class and among the farmers, not in the upper classes. To him, "the originative part of America" was "the part of America that makes new enterprises, the part into which the ambitious and gifted workingman makes his way up, the class that saves, that plans, that presently spreads its enterprises until they have a national scope and character." [1] It was this part of the population that he feared was being "squeezed out by the processes which we have been taught to call processes of prosperity." [2] The power of the great corporation was stifling and subordinating these creative average men, *the middle class*, even though prosperity was being brought by the corporation.

[1] Wilson, *op. cit.*, p. 17
[2] *Ibid.*, p. 17

This Wilson greatly feared, as would any democratic individualist.

Speaking of this middle class he said also: "Its members are sharing prosperity, no doubt, but what alarms me is that they are not *originating* prosperity. No country can afford to have its prosperity originated by a small controlling class. The treasury of America does not lie in the brains of a small body of men now in control of great enterprises that have been concentrated under the direction of a very small number of persons. The treasury of America lies in those ambitions, those energies, that cannot be restricted to a special favored class. It depends upon the inventions of unknown men, upon the originations of unknown men, upon the ambitions of unknown men. Every country is renewed out of the ranks of the unknown, not out of the ranks of those already famous and powerful and in control." [1]

It is doubtful whether in recent years many Americans have seriously faced the problem of the declining role of the individual and of the middle class, which is the main bulwark of individualism. True, we have become concerned over the apparent development of a power élite and the stifling effect of corporate organization on the initiative of men so that they become "organization men." There is also concern over the rights of the small stockholder in the large corporation, and the rights of the rank and file union member in the large union. But what is lacking is the Wilsonian type of concern, wherein a threat to liberty is regarded as a threat to the *very foundation of democracy itself.*

POWER AND FREEDOM

What is liberty anyway, and what is its companion, equality? Liberty, to be sure, is the absence of restraint. But restraint is restraint by someone. That someone was orig-

[1] *Ibid.*, pp. 17-18

inally the monarch. Today, large bodies like the great corporations, the government, and the unions provide the restraint. But why are bodies rather than individuals now the restraining forces? Why is Brown not as much of a restraining force on Jones, his neighbor, as is the corporation, the government, or the union? For the simple but very basic reason that Brown, as an individual, usually has little power over Jones because he is equal to Jones. If this were not the case, Brown could restrain Jones. Liberty or freedom arises mainly out of equality. But it is not equality in size or shape or intelligence that is important, but *equality in power. It is the inequality caused by the concentration of power that destroys liberty, equality, and individualism; and if democracy is regarded as the affirmation of individualism, concentrated power destroys democracy.*

The problem of democracy is thus the problem of concentrated power. As long as we had a socioeconomic situation in America that did not involve much power concentration, we had more democracy. Our main reason for fearing centralized power should be our fear for democracy. And if we do not object to a type of concentrated power that destroys freedom, we do not really want democracy. Moreover, we cannot convince the peoples of the world of the value of the democratic way of life if we do not really have it or want it. It is useless to think of ourselves as democratic if we accept, promote, and admire the concentration of power and do little or nothing to prevent its encroachment upon the rights and freedom of the individual.

What we have just said is not new. The gradual destruction of the freedom of the individual as a result of concentrated power and the decline of individualistic democracy has become increasingly apparent. Since the nineteenth century it has been realized (1) that democracy is the promotion of the freedom of the individual to develop his potentialities and to be governed only through consent; (2) that democracy is based on equality; (3) that equality and democracy are destroyed by organized, concentrated power; and (4) that the social losses involved are the destruction of individual freedom and serious social and economic imbalance. In the development of American society since 1860, concentration of power has violated these basic democratic truths and created a great power problem. To discover solutions for this problem is the main purpose of this book.

The destructive influence of the concentration of power, however, has never been fully understood. In the years after the Civil War, the common man's struggle against oppression by the power concentrates was vague and sporadic. Finally, in the administration of Franklin D. Roosevelt, the common man obtained political power. But even during and after the Roosevelt era, he lacked the main defense against the destructive influence of power—the socioeconomic theory that would explain its existence and democratize it.

Such a body of theory is of prime importance. If this book is to provide any viable solutions for the power problem, it can do so only by contributing to the development of such a theory. The construction and application of a new socioeconomic theory require a series of steps. (1) We need to trace the origins of the power problem and to trace the struggle against power. (2) We must see how certain answers began to emerge from the struggle and reveal their inadequacies. (3) With this background, and with modern social and economic analysis, we must construct a new socioeconomic theory. (4) We can then apply it to obtain solutions for the power problem. The solutions, we can state in advance, lie in planning under capitalism. This is the answer—*a new form of planning under capitalism.* But the justification as well as the explanation of the answer require a reexamination of the long political and theoretical road we have traveled since the injury to the individual from concentration of power was first perceived. The origins of the problem in economic changes, politics, and theory are the basis of creative reconstruction.

II

The Development of the Power Problem

THE beginnings of the American power problem can be traced to the differences which developed in our early history between the Federalists and the Republicans. The former represented the bankers, speculators, merchants, and manufacturers of the northern and central states; the latter, the agrarian interests generally, and especially the large plantation owners of the South. The leading protagonists in the struggle were Alexander Hamilton and Thomas Jefferson.

THE PROGRAMS OF HAMILTON AND JEFFERSON

Hamilton, our brilliant first Secretary of the Treasury, was a firm believer in credit and manufacturing as the means to national growth and prosperity. The dependence upon England, which was the major economic issue of the Revolutionary War, had to be broken permanently by the development of American industry behind tariff walls and by strong national credit. It was on Hamilton's efforts to refund the national debt, establish a national bank, and promote domestic manufacturing through protective tariffs that the issue between the two economic interests was first drawn.

Hamilton was far ahead of his times. He was convinced of what we now know, that a high standard of living depends on the growth of industrialism and the use of machine technology. Jefferson and his followers were opposed to the trend toward industrialism. Unlike Hamilton, they could not visualize the great dependence of wealth and income on mechanical processes. In addition, they feared the growth of cities and the power of bankers with a half-conscious realization that these threats to freedom presaged the end of the dominance of agriculture and of rural independence. It would seem that from their standpoint the revolution itself was a struggle against the encroachment of manufacturing and mercantile England upon the freedom of the farmers. These underlying attitudes aroused resentment toward the United States Bank, higher tariffs, and special excises to pay interest and principal on the refunded national and state debts, all cardinal elements in Hamilton's program.

The farm represented freedom: it provided independence. On the farm, food, shelter, and clothing could be obtained largely by one's own efforts. The sale of cotton and tobacco affected the degree of one's prosperity, but not one's existence. The farmer and the large plantation owner had not yet begun to worry about farm prices on the ground that if they were too low they would lose their farms and their livelihoods because of mortgage debts. Worry was directed rather toward what might be called outside tribute, in the form of taxes or prices for the goods that the farmer had to buy. To be sure, some farmers in the East and some of the southern planters were in debt, but the farm-debtor problem was not yet acute. That the farm could provide an independent living was not questioned. Firm and dear credit and the high taxes which Hamilton proposed were *external* threats to farmer independence. The farm itself meant freedom because it provided security and independence.

The farm meant freedom also because it involved no regulation. One could farm as he pleased so long as he did not harm others. The farm provided negative freedom in economic life. The elements of individual development that are involved in positive freedom were also present. Since great wealth or the great mass of consumers' goods we have today were not sought after, a man could hope to achieve his more limited needs for economic well-being by his own hard work and intelligence. He had the economic basis for self-development, or positive freedom.

But a form of social "statics" was involved. The good life on the farm was a static life, without any considerable or rapid social change. Out in vague space and created by God were invariable and enduring laws of nature. These laws were good and freedom lay in adhering to them. Since they were good and unchanging, man lived in the best of all possible societies when social life was organized according to natural law. He fulfilled himself completely by living according to nature. Since this was the best of all possible worlds, change was not only unnecessary; it was undesirable. It is easy to see why adherents of Jefferson were not attracted by the dynamic, forward-looking hopes of Hamilton. They had no zest for the growth of cities filled with new factories —or even for a change in farming.

Hamilton saw things differently. His ambitions for the future were outlined in the *Report on Manufactures* (December 5, 1791). This unique document is the beginning of what might be called national economics and had great influence on subsequent thought, not only in this country but in Germany and other continental countries. Industry was to be fostered behind tariff walls and through public subsidy. As a result, machinery could be more extensively utilized, groups not otherwise employed—such as women and children—could be employed; immigration could increase; and many opportunities for talent and skill could appear. The farmer was to benefit from the resulting growth in population and the greater need for food and agricultural products. Hamilton did not regard his program as one that interfered with agriculture, but as a benefit to it.

Over the years, the real basis of the difference between Hamilton and Jefferson has been distorted by overemphasizing the controversy between free trade and protectionism. Far more significant than mere protectionism was Hamilton's belief that national welfare depended upon the growth of industry, upon urban life, and upon the increase of population. Hamilton was not only attacking the rural philosophy of Jefferson; he was advocating vigorous economic dynamism. He was for change, and, as it turned out, for power and materialism. He was not concerned with liberty or individualism. He was seeking the growth of production of *things. He was seeking power over nature and men.*

With the election of Jefferson in 1800, the voters had decided to oppose the dynamic proposals of Hamilton. Voting strength lay with the farmers, and the Federalists failed to convince them that the growth of business enterprise was in their interest if higher taxes and consumer prices were required to achieve it. Business enterprise was not yet strong enough of itself to get its way. There then followed a number of years in which the struggle was not acute, in which business bowed to the will of the majority. The fear of Jefferson that his election might mean the disruption of the Union was not realized, and men accepted the obligation expressed by Jefferson to abide by the will of the majority.[1]

AGRICULTURAL DYNAMIC MATERIALISM

The administration of Jefferson did not, however, remain true to the principles of a static and freedom-loving agrarianism. The force of events and the desires of some of Jefferson's adherents led them to the substitution of an agrarian material dynamism for the industrial material dynamism of Hamilton. In later days, support of agriculture was not in terms of preserving an Arcadian, idyllic, static mode of life.

[1] *Cf.* the First Inaugural Address

It became an aggressive struggle for more and better land in the Southwest and in Canada. Although Jeffersonians had prided themselves on a strict interpretation of the Constitution and restriction of the Federal Government to a modest role, agrarian aggressiveness and the change in the balance of power in Europe made them favor even stronger national action than did the Federalists. It is apparent that neither the planter nor the small farmer was content to live a life of static rural freedom when the opportunity of bettering himself and his family lay in westward expansion or in the greater sale of cotton abroad. The planters saw the area of the great Southwest as room for the expansion of the slave system. The small farmer saw the West as an area where he could get better land.

When conflict arose again in 1828 over the adoption of a high tariff, it was of a very different character than the earlier one over the Hamilton program. It was not a struggle of the planter and poor farmer to prevent taxation for the benefit of business enterprise. It was, instead, a struggle between conflicting enterprise interests. The planters and successful farmers were selling surpluses of cotton, tobacco, and other products abroad. The tariff not only increased the price of the products which American farmers had to purchase; it reduced the sale of farmers' produce abroad. Foreign trade over long periods is a balance of commodity trade. The purchase of our goods depends upon our willingness to purchase the goods of other countries.[1] Stoppage of the free flow of British goods to the United States hampered the flow of our agricultural products to England. It was not in the interest of the planters to see American industry grow. The sale of cotton for British textiles was far more important in volume than its sale for American textiles. The planter

---

[1] Senator McDuffie of South Carolina argued bluntly as early as 1830 that southern cotton could only be sold in exchange for the manufactured goods of Great Britain.

preferred to be a supplier of raw material to British industry, since British industry bought most of his product.

The conflict over the tariff, the rates of which had risen to forty percent in 1829, was resolved by Clay's compromise of 1833, but not without bitter controversy, nullification, and the threat of South Carolina to secede. The tariff battle continued, however, and succeeded for a while in splitting the Republican party into a Democratic party following Jackson and Van Buren, and a Whig party headed by Henry Clay.

THE WHIGS AND THE CLAY COMPROMISE

The Whigs favored the continuance of the United States Bank, the maintenance of moderately protective tariffs, and the improvement of transportation connecting the East and the West. The program supported by Clay proposed for the first time to unite the interests of the small western farmers with those of the eastern manufacturers. The new party attracted the many enemies made by Jackson in his first term of office. To the Whig standard came friends of the national bank, believers in sound money, merchants, manufacturers, and business men, as well as many small and some large farmers of the South and West. Ideologically, the leaders of the new party developed a philosophy known as the National System, which closely approximated the original views of Hamilton. It represented a return to Hamilton's belief that the welfare and future growth of the country depended upon the increase of manufacturing behind tariff protection. Like Hamilton, its supporters argued that industrial growth was in the interest of the farmer. More stress was laid on the development of roads and public works than in the earlier period, however. The Whig standard bearer, Henry Clay, was defeated by Jackson in 1832, but the party finally succeeded in electing Harrison and Tyler in 1840.

The power struggle in the time of the Whigs thus consisted of a new effort by the Hamiltonians to obtain power for the sake of American business. As in Hamilton's day, the Whigs attempted to "sell" the farmers on the belief that protectionism was good for them. But the effort again proved a failure.

The union of small farmers and northern industrialists might have been easier to accomplish had it not been for the issue raised by the United States Bank. The farmers were rapidly becoming a debtor class. They needed loans to purchase land and to tide them over years of poor crops. The Bank did not meet their needs. It stood for restricted loans and sound currency. Jackson, in his second term, had made great political capital out of the Bank issue. Violently he had accused it of charging high interest to the farmers for the benefit of its stockholders, who were mainly from the northeastern states. The poor farmer and artisan were led to believe that the Bank created a money monopoly which made it difficult for them to obtain credit. Thus President Tyler, who had succeeded Harrison, so feared the opposition of the poor farmers that he was unwilling to adopt Clay's proposal for the restoration of a strong national bank. When Clay succeeded in getting two bank bills through Congress, Tyler vetoed them. Tyler proved to be right, and Clay's support of the Bank lost the Whigs the votes of the small farmers who had been largely responsible for the election of Harrison.

In the election of Polk in 1844, the overwhelming majority of agrarian voters who had supported Jefferson and Jackson returned to what was known by then as the Democratic party. The Whigs could not build a popular party which was capable of winning a majority. They could not gain the support of either the large or the small farmers. Without the support of substantial numbers of both, the Hamiltonian program could not be restored.

After 1844 the power of the agrarian groups became entrenched. Not until the Civil War were they to be divided,

making possible the capture of Congress by men favorable
to business enterprise. In the meantime, agrarian dynamism dominated the country. With the push south and
westward into Texas and California, people were preoccupied with a vague belief in Manifest Destiny. Vigorous
and active, they felt that an expansion south to the Rio
Grande and west to the Pacific was not only their right, but
their foreordained goal. The struggle for power was thus
turned outward. It was a fight for land against Indians and
Mexicans, and it was also a bitter struggle against nature
and for gold.

Superficially, the country was united. The Democratic
party controlled both Presidency and Congress with the
election of Franklin Pierce. The vast majority of the voters
were in favor of a low tariff and opposed to shipping subsidies, internal improvement financed by the Federal Government, the Bank, and the increase in the federal debt. Moreover, the majority accepted slavery. Bitter differences were
developing, of course, over the extension of slavery into the
territories, but even at the time of the election of Abraham
Lincoln the abolitionists constituted only a small proportion
of the total population.

THE CIVIL WAR

Underneath the surface of this apparent unity were vast
changes leading to the fundamental differences fought over
in the Civil War. These changes were mainly economic.
They consisted of the growth of a large body of small farmers operating with nonslave labor, the growth of manufacturing and industrialism, the great increase in the laboring
class, the appearance of large cities, and the beginnings of
railroad transportation from east to west.

Instead of a society consisting of large planters and small
farmers who overwhelmingly outnumbered the merchants
and manufacturers of the North, there had developed a three-

part sectional division. First, there were the planters surrounded by pro-slave small farmers in the Deep South and in the border states of Kentucky, North Carolina, Virginia, and Maryland. Then there were the merchants, manufacturers, workers, and small free farmers of the East; and finally there were the western free farmers of Ohio, Illinois, California, and the northern territories. The manufactured products of the East had become of vast importance. By 1859 they amounted to $1,900,000,000, whereas the agricultural products of the South (cotton, tobacco, rice, and sugar) were valued at only $204,000,000, little more than a tenth as much.

The plantation system itself had changed. By the time of the tariff compromise of 1833, it had become an aggressive form of business enterprise, selling its goods to England and the continent and requiring free trade so that these goods could be paid for by the importation of manufactured goods from abroad. This change came about from the invention of the cotton gin, which enabled a slave to clean fifty times more cotton per day than he could clean by hand labor. Cheap cotton resulted, but this required the growth and sale of many times as much cotton. In turn, the need for volume meant (1) larger and larger plantations, and movement westward to virgin land; and (2) greater dependence on the foreign market, since the northern mills could not buy all the cotton. Cotton farming had become big business, requiring more and more land and slaves and depending increasingly on foreign trade.

By the time of the Civil War, however, the cotton plantation system had begun to break down. The exhaustion of the land and the high cost of slave labor greatly reduced profit margins. The planters could not afford even moderately high tariffs, and since they controlled Congress, tariffs had been reduced in the administrations of both Pierce and Buchanan. A change of government bringing about the raising of tariffs or restriction of the expansion of slavery into the West would have ruined the planters.

Accompanying these economic changes were changes in the class structure of American society. The planters had become a wealthy and arrogant aristocracy believing in a feudalistic way of life. The small farmers who had once been content to live subserviently alongside the planter aristocracy had become a more numerous and self-respecting group, spreading into the Middle West. They had achieved a degree of social status under Jackson and by the time of the Civil War had risen much further in income and power. In addition, a powerful urban middle class had developed, consisting of merchants and manufacturers who were now the wealthiest people in the nation. They were impatient to take political power out of the hands of the planters, who still dominated politics even though they had lost their economic dominance.

In short, the power balance had changed, and this change was to be recognized, rather than caused, by the Civil War. It is one of the greatest tragedies—if not the greatest—of American history that this political change was not or could not be effected by a peaceful transition such as occurred in England when the Liberals, representing the industrial middle class, superseded the Tories of the landed aristocracy, through elections.

A major reason for the violence of the transition was the political ambivalence of the western farmer. As has been indicated, Clay, like Hamilton, had failed to convince the small farmer that his economic interest lay in high tariffs and the growth of manufacturing. As a result, the small farmer had remained in the Democratic party supporting the interests of the planter, and the break was delayed until the election of 1860. Even then, it occurred not because of any strong conviction that his interests lay with the manufacturers, but because he believed that he could no longer support the expansion of the slave system into the West, where it competed for the land he wanted to use. The new Republican party, by opposing slavery in the territories, got part of the small-farmer vote. Part of the Democratic party got the rest by supporting squatter sovereignty.

The result of the rift in the Democratic party and the loss of the small-farmer vote was the election of Lincoln, and a Congress which represented only a minority of the voters. The new government was committed again to Hamiltonian policies, a high tariff, subsidies to shipping and railroads, and internal improvements. Although it is hazardous to speculate as to what might have happened without the Civil War, it would seem that a majority of the small farmers still could not have been convinced that their interests lay with the manufacturers. Had the war not occurred, they might have yet resisted a Hamiltonian program. But the war precluded further vacillation. When South Carolina seceded and Beauregard attacked Fort Sumter, the die was cast; the passions of both North and South were hopelessly aroused; and the old fear of disruption of the Union upon which national security depended became a powerful force. Northern small farmers were then convinced by noneconomic motives that their interests lay with the manufacturers not only in the preservation of the Union but in the destruction of slavery and the plantation system.

Thus the war became a second American revolution. It was "a social war, ending in the unquestioned establishment of a new power in the government, making vast changes in the arrangement of classes, in the accumulation and distribution of wealth, in the course of industrial development, and in the Constitution inherited from the Fathers." [1] The war destroyed the economic and social system of the South and insured the rule of the manufacturing interests in Washington for more than sixty years. As a result, *the Federal*

1 Beard, C. and M., *The Rise of American Civilization*, vol. II, p. 53

Government became an active force in stimulating business and ultimately in creating big business and monopoly. Along with the industrial revolution, it was a basic cause of the concentration of power and the destruction of democracy and individualism. The war hastened the triumph of big business, materialism, and the concentration of power in the hands of a few.

III

The Revolt Against the
Concentration of Power

A REVOLT against the great concentration of power which threatened individual and public welfare was inevitable. It developed soon after the Civil War and had as its main current the agrarian reformism of the Middle West. Two other less vigorous currents were (1) the middle-class reform movements, in the cities against graft and boss rule, and on the national level against the patronage system and the tariff "pork barrel"; and (2) the rise of the labor movement with its political implications. On the whole, the backbone of revolt was the opposition of the farmers, culminating in the progressive movement of 1910.

In the beginning, the chief complaint of farmers had to do with their treatment by the railroads, which were charging high rates for transportation and storage facilities. Sporadic movements began for the state regulation of railroad rates. The many farmers' clubs, the "Patrons of Husbandry," although not originally political, became increasingly interested in the "railroad problem" and in other reforms. They finally participated actively in politics.

THE LIBERAL REPUBLICANS AND THE GRANGERS

The actual political beginning of the revolt on a national scale, however, was the defection of the Liberal Wing of the

Republican party in 1872. This group nominated Horace Greeley to run in the presidential election against Ulysses S. Grant. In this move, Liberal Republicans were supported by the weak and broken Democratic party. Although the main concern of many of the Liberals was the failure to return suffrage privileges to former Confederates, the Liberal platform supported lower tariffs, the regulation of the railroads, and the personal income tax. The Liberal Party movement declined with the overwhelming election of Grant to a second term in 1872, but it persisted for some years in such states as Illinois, Ohio, Michigan, and Missouri. In the years after 1872, it was mainly concerned with preventing a third term for General Grant.

More fundamental in the beginnings of the revolt were the Granger parties. These represented a genuine farmers' movement against the controlling group in the Capital and were organized in various states under such names as "Independent," "Reform," and "Anti-Monopoly" parties. They concentrated on the regulation of railroads and the enactment of state antitrust laws. The original cause of their formation was the overexpansion of wheat and corn production in such middle western states as Illinois, Iowa, Wisconsin, and Minnesota. The railroads were unable to handle the large production of grain, which at that time greatly exceeded domestic demand. The results were falling grain prices and rising railroad rates. The Granger parties flourished from 1873 to 1875, and elected a number of representatives to Congress.

The Grangers succeeded in getting the enactment of state laws establishing commissions in Illinois, Iowa, Wisconsin, and other states, to investigate and later to regulate railroad rates in intrastate commerce. At first the power of the commissions to regulate rates was challenged in the courts, and some of the laws were repealed, only to be reenacted a few years later. But this power was finally upheld by the Supreme

Court in the case of *Munn vs. Illinois*. It then remained to pass legislation to regulate rates in interstate commerce, and the movement which began in these early days finally succeeded in the enactment of the Interstate Commerce Law of 1887.

THE RISE OF MONEY POLITICS

Significant for our purposes here was the increasing interest after 1873 in the problems created by the gold standard and the downward trend in prices which persisted from 1873 to 1896. This price trend was to play a major role in the fight against monopoly and the power of business, by all levels of government.

The downward price trend was particularly damaging to farmers, who saw their fixed debt obligations becoming heavier and the prices of crops with which to pay off debt falling. As a result, farm politics shifted from railroad to money politics.

To the untutored man on the farm or in the factory, there seemed to be a shortage of money. Ample supplies of "greenback" money had appeared during the Civil War and continued to circulate after the war. The greenbacks had raised farm prices. What was more natural than that there should arise a clamor for the issue of more of this green money? But Congress vacillated over the future of the greenbacks. A total of $350 million in greenbacks had been issued during the Civil War. In 1866 the "sound money" forces passed a redemption act which called for a reduction of this issue at the rate of $4,000,000 a month. The "cheap money" forces prevailed in 1868, however, and the act was repealed. Again in 1878 the scene changed and the sound-money forces triumphed by passing an act to cut the size of the issue to $346 million.

The defeat of the "greenbackers" in Congress led to the organization of a Greenback party. In 1876, a convention was held in Indianapolis which nominated Peter Cooper for President. He received only 80,000 votes. The movement, however, gathered force after the Greenback party allied itself with the so-called Labor Reform party in 1878, and the resulting "National" party, still popularly called the Greenback party, received over a million votes in state and congressional elections.[1] But this was the high water mark of the greenback movement. In 1880, with high hopes, the greenbackers nominated General James B. Weaver of Iowa for the Presidency. But despite a platform which expanded their program to include general economic reforms as well as cheap money, they succeeded in polling only 300,000 votes.

By 1882, many of the independents who had voted for the third parties turned to the Democratic party. Elements favoring cheap money, antitrust laws, civil service reform, low tariffs, the income tax, and many other liberal measures began to form a sizeable left wing in this party. What with many liberal defections from the Republican party, there was a Democratic landslide in the congressional elections of 1882, and the trend continued, resulting in the election of Cleveland in 1884.

THE FREE SILVER MOVEMENT

The years 1884 to 1888 witnessed several abortive attempts to organize labor politically, but, as we have pointed out, the backbone of the attack on business power before the turn of the century continued to be the opposition represented by the individualistic and democratic farmer. After a brief period of some improvement in farm prosperity, farming became increasingly unprofitable. Farm difficulties were especially acute in the South and the Middle West, and again the problems were attributed to falling prices, tight credit, and the scarcity of money. The gold standard became the villain. With silver now a much more plentiful metal, and

[1] Cf. Haynes, F. E., *Social Politics in the United States*, p. 161

with western congressmen concerned to promote the silver interests, the demand for cheap money shifted from a demand for more greenbacks to a demand for the restoration of bimetallism and the free coinage of silver. Silver coinage had been abolished by what Bryan called the "crime of 1873," the dropping of the silver dollar from the free coinage list.

The clamor for silver currency in the South and the West assumed the nature of a religious crusade. New farmers' organizations, called Alliances, appeared and greatly aided in the silver campaign. Like the earlier Grangers, they were not originally political, but they very soon turned to state and national action and espoused especially the cause of free silver. They were to become powerful, electing three governors, one United States senator, and thirty congressmen. By 1890, farmers had been aroused to great anger against gold money and to a lesser extent against the high tariff and monopoly. As a result, in the congressional elections of 1890, the House of Representatives was captured by the Democrats, and the representatives of the disaffected voters succeeded in passing a silver purchase act.

Although the anti-monopoly movement was not at the center of the farm struggle for power in 1890, a by-product of the struggle was the passage of the Sherman Antitrust Act. In this the farmer was aided by a miscellaneous group of "small" people in the cities who were increasingly concerned over the growing concentration of economic power and large fortunes. Countless individuals were injured by the activities of business monopolies. Between 1879 and 1890, trusts had been formed with over a billion dollars of assets in such fields as oil refining, sugar refining, cordage, and whiskey. To some extent the trusts were the result of cut-throat competition, the general decline in prices, the desire of investment banks to obtain large promoters' profits, and the visions of high profits in the minds of those who had part interest in the trusts. The idea of combination through the device of turning over corporate voting stock to a board of voting trustees has been attributed to a number of people, but undoubtedly its most famous "inventor" was John D. Rockefeller. The trust was an ideal form of combination because it was simple and stable and avoided attack from the common law against conspiracy in restraint of trade.

The Sherman Antitrust Law of 1890 was a very short document, prohibiting contracts, combinations, and conspiracies in restraint of trade. Persons who monopolized or attempted to monopolize, combine or conspire were guilty of misdemeanors. There were criminal penalties consisting of fines and prison terms, and a civil penalty in terms of a suit by injured parties for triple damages.

THE POPULISTS AND THE FREE SILVER DEMOCRATS

In 1892, farmer opposition to business control took yet another form. A new Populist party was organized through the influence of farmer alliances and other groups. In its presidential convention of 1892, General Weaver, the former Greenback candidate, was nominated as the standard bearer. As in 1880, he conducted a vigorous personal campaign, going from town to town throughout the rural areas. The results were gratifying: again a third party received over a million popular votes. The campaign contributed to the defeat of Harrison and the reelection of the Democrat Cleveland. Most of the votes came from the western and southern states.

Throughout Cleveland's second administration, revolt and unrest grew, turning more voters toward the new Populist party. The farm movement against Washington gained strength for a number of reasons. Among these were (1) the repeal of the Sherman Silver Act, (2) the failure of Richard Olney, Cleveland's Attorney General, to enforce the Antitrust Law vigorously against business although cases were brought against unions,[1] (3) the serious depression of 1893, (4) the continued fall in farm prices, (5) the failure of the Congress to live up to the promises of the Democrats to reduce tariffs, and (6) the insistence of Cleveland on preserving the gold standard at any cost.

In 1896 the Democratic party was captured by the free silver movement, and the Populist party merged with it, both accepting Bryan as their candidate. From this time until 1910, the major issues before the country were fought out within the two major parties.

THE LABOR MOVEMENT AND HENRY GEORGE

The labor movement, along with agrarian movements, slowly and belatedly played its part in the struggle against concentrated power. There was little political organization of labor in the nineteenth century. The first national organization, the National Labor Union, however, espoused the cause of the Greenbackers and organized a weak workingman's party, the National Reform party. The subsequent Knights of Labor ventured into politics from time to time. But the organization which ultimately became the basic and successful national body, the American Federation of Labor, in 1886, confined itself largely to questions of wages and hours. It stayed aloof from permanent affiliation with any party, and sought its political ends—especially aid to education and various kinds of labor and social legislation —mainly through bargaining with the two major parties. One important exception was the adoption, on the insistence of the American Federation of Labor, of eight labor planks in the Populist party platform in the election of 1892. However, union membership undoubtedly swelled the vote of the Greenbackers, the Populists, and especially the Democratic party in 1882 and 1896. But the numerous weak and sporadic

[1] The first business case of any significance was the E. C. Knight Sugar Trust case of 1893.

workingmen's parties had little influence except for occasional successes in state and local elections.

Along the sidelines of farmer progressivism must also be placed the reformist influence of the Henry George movement. It is hard to assess the role of Henry George. His book *Progress and Poverty* and the teachings of his followers impressed many with the belief that American industrialism was creating great and unwarranted inequality of wealth. But attention was focused on the enormous increments of urban land value rather than upon the control of Congress by business, especially big business. The Henry George movement, however, did arouse some of the discontent with capitalism as it was then operating, and increased interest in tax reform. After going to England and Ireland, where his proposals for land reform were enthusiastically applauded, George returned to New York with much heightened prestige. Gradually he broadened his reformist views and became very active in the politics of New York City. He was twice an unsuccessful candidate for mayor, dying of apoplexy during the second campaign. He was strongly supported by labor and became a symbol of the attack upon monopolistic power and the "evils" of the gold standard.

THE PROGRESSIVE MOVEMENT OF 1910

Real success in the efforts of the average man to curb the concentration of economic and political power began with the progressive movement in 1910. It was the result of groundwork done in Wisconsin by the elder La Follette. According to Senator Dolliver, La Follette was one of the first congressmen "to comprehend the character of the irrepressible conflict . . . between public interests and the present-day organization of private business." [1] With La Follette, there was not just vague opposition to business power. The problem was clearly and openly defined. Business was def-

[1] Haynes, *op. cit.*, p. 169

initely accused of acting against the public interest and of destroying the rights and freedom of individuals.

Along with La Follette, liberals in states other than Wisconsin were active in building the progressive movement in the years from 1890 to 1910. Among the leading Progressives were H. S. Pingree, Samuel M. Jones, Tom L. Johnson, William S. U'Ren and Joseph W. Folk. In Wisconsin and other middle western states the fight was much the same. It was against bossism and political corruption, and it attacked privileged groups and big business as the causes of corruption (the so-called invisible government). It favored greater regulation of railroads, the return of government control to the people through the direct primary, the referendum, the recall, and the direct popular election of United States senators. The movement was definitely against monopoly and big business. It was aided by writers like William Allen White and Lincoln Steffens, who described the scandalous tactics of big business in causing political corruption.

By chance, however, Theodore Roosevelt, rather than La Follette, became the great protagonist of progressivism. To use a colloquialism, he "stole the show," and not so much by intent as by the mysterious power of politics to mold a man to its needs of the hour.

Roosevelt became a national hero as a result of the charge on San Juan Hill. It was natural that he should enter politics. But when he did, the political bosses were uneasy. He made unguarded statements. Beard quotes a letter of Roosevelt to Lodge in 1897 in which he said, in part, "The really ugly feature of the Republican canvas is that it does represent what the Populists say, that is, corrupt wealth. . . ." [1] In those days of agitation, the New York bosses Platt and Tracy were willing to take chances in order to put forward a candidate of integrity, although they were never too happy with Roose-

[1] Cf. Beard, op. cit., vol. II, p. 425

velt as Governor or as the nominee for Vice-President in 1900. But when McKinley was assassinated and Roosevelt became President, very little occurred in his first administration that was discouraging to business. Neither his policies nor his utterances as President were disturbing. At one point, Roosevelt said, "We are neither for the rich man as such nor the poor man as such; we are for the upright man, rich or poor." [1] Instead of taking legal action against monopoly, he favored the use of adverse publicity. Railway rates, he said, should be "just." The natural resources "should be conserved." But nothing of any consequence happened, and he was nominated for a full term as President with the confidence of even the conservatives who controlled the party, such as Aldrich, Cannon, and Hanna.

By 1905, however, Roosevelt began to move toward vigorous progressivism. He was the first President to attempt really to enforce the antitrust law. He got through a pure food and drug act, and he strengthened the powers of the Interstate Commerce Commission. Most extreme, he favored income and inheritance taxes. By 1908, he was rapidly taking the place of La Follette as the leader of the Progressives. His chosen successor, William Howard Taft, was pledged to continue his policies. Both Taft and the public thought this would happen. But Taft was not the man for the job. A rift with Roosevelt developed, and the latter accused him of failing to pursue progressivism. Actually Taft made a good record in the attack upon monopoly, but he would sometimes allow conservative members of Congress to have their way on other issues important to progressives. Eventually he took the middle road and sought a compromise between the two wings of his party. In this he failed. By 1912, the split in the Republican ranks had resulted in control of Congress by the Democrats, and many Republicans believed that Taft should not be renominated.

[1] Beard, *op. cit.*, vol. II, p. 597

The split in the Republican party between Taft and Roosevelt resulted in the formation of the Progressive party. The national convention to form the new party was held on August 15, 1912. It was a turbulent and unconventional affair, with a crusading spirit. The delegates sang "Onward Christian Soldiers" and the "Battle Hymn of the Republic." A prominent social worker, Jane Addams, had a leading role in the deliberations, something unheard of in politics. A platform was adopted with strong planks for industrial health, accident insurance, child-labor laws, minimum wages, regulation of women's labor, maximum hours for men, industrial education and research, vigorous action against monopolies, protection of children, and many other social reforms. Miss Addams assured the public that the party had become "the American exponent of a worldwide movement toward just social conditions." In short, the party had become not only an attack upon the control by big business in Washington, but the rallying point for the most advanced nonsocialist liberalism in the United States.

But the split thus created in the Republican ranks insured the election of Woodrow Wilson. Although the combined votes of Taft and Roosevelt constituted a majority of the popular vote, the seemingly more moderate Wilson gained an overwhelming majority of the electoral vote. Much of Wilson's support came from those favoring the middle of the road between Taft and Roosevelt.

THE PLIGHT OF THE COMMON MAN

The period of the revolt against concentrated power from 1872 to 1910 should not be thought of simply in terms of political movements against a Republican party which represented business interests during those years. One should not lose sight of the cause of the revolt, the declining position of the common man. The farmers, workers, and small business men all suffered from the effects of industrialism and concentrated power, and constituted a complex group of ordinary men whose relative social, political, and economic status steadily diminished. Although their problems differed, all shared in losses of power, equality, democracy, and independence. The significance and nature of the revolt can be clarified by a description of the plight of the common man in each of the three groups.

Let us begin with the farmers. From the time of Jefferson to the Civil War, small farmers obtained the suffrage, acquired a great deal of individual security, experienced for the most part a rising standard of living, moved in many cases to better land in Ohio, Indiana, Illinois, Iowa, and other middlewestern states, and achieved a great deal of social equality due to the philosophy of the Jacksonian period. Although the planter aristocracy grew in power and wealth, the millions of small farmers also made great gains.

The Civil War and the growth of industrialism reversed this upward trend for large sections of the agricultural population. In the the first place, the war broke the plantation system. Southern farmers, both large and small, suffered poverty and loss of influence. Cotton farming was no longer profitable. It had begun to become depressed before the war. The northern and western farmers also suffered economic difficulties. Agricultural machinery and the use of new land tended to create an oversupply of the basic grains, wheat and corn. Prices fell between 1873 and 1896. Farmers as a group were already mainly debtors and they now went even more heavily into debt. They found interest payments increasingly burdensome. In addition, farmers were plagued by rising costs of transportation and grain storage. The high cost of farm machinery was another problem.

Instead of independence, the growing commercial character of farming made the farmer more dependent. His security was endangered by the power of the railroads, the sellers of machinery, and the banks that held his mortgages. Since he sold his grain and livestock in competitive markets, prices of these products tended to fall below industrial prices. The latter could be stabilized or raised through monopolistic methods. Thus the farmer suffered a relative loss in purchasing power.

Instead of maintaining equality, the farmer lost status to the business man in the cities. Relative to the rising tycoons of business, he became far inferior. He found that wealthy men were able to exercise much greater influence on Congress and the state legislatures than he could, not only as an individual, but even in organized groups. He still retained his freedom to control his farm, but this negative freedom failed to provide him with the economic equality and power he needed to retain his former level in society.

The plight of the growing working class in cities was worse. Although wages rose due to the shortage of labor, the working man had no economic security. Depressions could wipe out his small savings and create dire want. Working conditions were often bad and the hours of work long. His wages failed to rise as rapidly as profits and entrepreneurial incomes. He bargained with thousands of other workers for wages and jobs against a few employers. As businesses grew large, he became increasingly dependent upon employers. Politically, he had little power compared with wealthy business men. He had even less control over working conditions in the factory than he had in politics. His working life was rigidly controlled by his employers, since they owned the mechanical means of production. The worker, to sum it up, suffered loss of individual freedom and equality because of lack of industrial democracy, social insurance protection, minimum wage laws, and social legislation in general. The growing size and concentration of control in business made it increasingly difficult to obtain freedom, equality, or independence through individual action. Even political equality was impaired by the concentration of power.

The small businessman was less injured by these nine-teenth-century changes than was the farmer or worker. But toward the end of the period, he, also, began to suffer. He had to face the growing competition of big businesses and monopolies and falling prices in competitive markets. Even before the depression of 1929, many small enterprisers deserted the Republican party to support the movements for free silver, antitrust legislation, and lower tariffs.

As we turn now to the developments after 1912, we must not forget these real personal bases for the struggle against concentrated power. The common men who opposed this power were real and sentient human beings who saw them-selves forced down by power concentrates so that they be-came increasingly insecure, unequal, and politically im-potent. The idyllic, static, natural-laws basis for democracy in the independent owner-operated farm or business had been largely destroyed. Nearly half the population were no longer farmers and many farmers had become tenants. The great movement to the cities, the commercialization of farming, the factory system, the growth in the size of businesses, the giant corporation, the growing inequality of wealth, and the great monopolies and semimonopolies had destroyed the Jef-fersonian basis of democracy. Nothing had taken its place. Nothing yet has fully taken its place.

IV

The New Freedom

THUS far our historical sketch of the shift to dynamic materialism, the rise of concentrated power, and the destruction of individualism and democracy has revealed a number of basic political movements and changes. (1) Until the Civil War, the small farmers and planters united to control the Federal Government in the interest of agrarian materialism and frustrated the growth of urban industrial materialism. (2) The Civil War, however, turned over the Federal Government to the northern industrialists, and speeded industrialism. The war and the industrial revolution soon led to a concentration of power which began to destroy individualism and damage individual welfare. (3) As a result, a revolt—led mainly by the farmers—began against the concentration of power. (4) But until the election of Theodore Roosevelt and the development of the Progressive movement, no real progress was made in curbing the concentration of power. (5) The efforts of the Greenbackers, Grangers, free-silverites, socialist labor parties, Georgeites, and Populists were sporadic and resulted in little more than the passage of the Interstate Commerce and Antitrust Acts. They represented merely a vague revolt against concentrated power which had no basic philosophy behind it, and no general social theory that would explain how individualism and democracy could be restored.

The progressive movement created the first comprehensive social philosophies supporting the welfare of the individual in an economy of concentrated power. In the election of 1912 these philosophies took shape and were called the *New Nationalism* and the *New Freedom*.

As we have pointed out, the split between the Taft Republicans and the Progressives insured the election of Woodrow Wilson in 1912. He was regarded at first as more moderate than Roosevelt because he was critical of the liberals in both parties. But as the campaign developed, his views appeared to be similar to those of Roosevelt. Both were against privilege and for the vigorous enforcement of the antitrust laws. Both were for more extensive regulation of the railroads and the establishment of a central banking system. Some slight difference appeared over the tariff, in that Wilson came out flatly for a lower tariff and tried to center his campaign around this issue, whereas Roosevelt supported a tariff which would equalize American and foreign costs of production. As the campaign reached a climax, however, broad philosophical differences between the two men began to appear. Roosevelt supported a nationalistic philosophy which he called The New Nationalism and Wilson advocated a contrasting individualistic philosophy, The New Freedom.

In essence, the New Nationalism of Roosevelt was a combination of governmental centralism and what in more recent times has been called the Welfare State. The influences bearing on him were those of Herbert Croly [1] and a strong group of politically-minded social workers led by Jane Addams. Croly contended that the division in American politics between Hamiltonism and Jeffersonism should be reversed. Hamilton had favored strong central government on behalf of the propertied and privileged groups. The followers of Jefferson favored the common man, but were for weak central government. The time had now come, Croly wrote, for the

[1] Author of a widely read book, *The Promise of American Life*

party of the common man to favor strong central government in behalf of the common man. Add to this view the social legislation urged by the social workers, and the opposition of the progressives generally to monopoly, privilege, big business, railroads, and high tariffs, and we have the substance of the New Nationalism.

To many of these views Wilson found himself opposed. He was not willing to abandon economic competition. He was not willing to accept the trusts as inevitable, although he believed that big business was inevitable in fields where it was genuinely more efficient than small business. He regarded the widespread adoption of social welfare legislation as a form of state paternalism which he considered dangerous and destructive of the American way of life. He favored the rights of the average man, but he was not very friendly to unionism. In fact, his subsequent equivocal position on the application of the antitrust laws to unions lost him the support of Samuel Gompers.

But the New Freedom was not merely a critique of the New Nationalism, lacking any positive elements. It was not merely an attempt to retain and restore competition, and it was most certainly not a doctrine of laissez-faire and localism. Wilson left office with the Federal Government vastly more powerful and regulatory than it had ever been. What is crucial in the ideas of the New Freedom was Wilson's belief in *competition as an ideal,* or, it might be said, *the results or effects of competition as an ideal.* Wilson was not opposed to the regulation of business in the general interest, nor did he think it possible to abolish big business and re-create an economy of small competitive enterprise. What the New Freedom proposed was the regulation of business in such a way as to restore the protective *effects* of competition.

Many voters regarded Wilson as more general and less specific than Roosevelt, and it may be that some voted for him simply because they did not believe that his administration would mean sweeping changes. But the years 1913 to 1915 saw more fundamental new legislation passed than in any two previous years in American history. Wilson and his followers were men of action, even though in their campaigning they had seemed less practical and specific than their opponents.

Wilson was also a public leader, one of the greatest this country has ever had. He was not content to follow public opinion. He sought to convert it to his ideals. It is well known that Wilson believed strongly in responsible party government. He was determined to become the leader and spokesman of the Democratic party, and to control Congress rather than to act merely as the head of the executive branch of the Government. With a comfortable majority in both houses, with a great many new liberal Democratic congressmen, and with a general desire on the part of the Democrats to "make good," he had little difficulty in organizing Congress behind his program, in spite of the conservatism of some of the older southern members.

The beginnings of the implementation of the New Freedom came when Wilson called a special session of Congress on April 8, 1913 to consider a new tariff. He broke precedent by coming to Congress personally to read a message of recommendations. After many preliminary hearings and frequent conferences between the President and Oscar Underwood, the Underwood-Simmons Tariff Act was passed. It was the first reform and nonprivilege tariff since 1861. It lowered the average tariff rates from forty to twenty-four percent, eliminated many privileged tariffs, and put many items on the free list, including (against strong opposition) both wool and sugar. The rates on agricultural machinery and many consumers' goods were greatly reduced.

Attached to the tariff measure in anticipation of a loss of revenue from the lower rates was an income tax measure sponsored by Cordell Hull. The federal income tax had become constitutional with the ratification of the Sixteenth Amendment on February 25, 1913. The new tax proposal was a modest one, allowing exemptions of $3,500 for single persons and $4,000 for married couples. Rates were graduated from one to three percent. The lack of progressivity in the tax aroused violent opposition from Senator La Follette and other Progressives. They wanted a maximum rate of ten percent and the inclusion of an inheritance tax of seventy-five percent.

But the objections of the Progressives to the low income-tax rates were the least of the difficulties faced by the new tariff bill. A group of conservative Democratic senators opposed tariff-free sugar and wool importation. In addition, lobbies for various other interests descended on Washington in droves. At this point, the popular will seemed to be on the verge of defeat again. In previous tariff actions, reformist lower tariffs passed by the House had been raised by business interests exerting pressure in the Senate. Wilson made personal appeals to recalcitrant senators and finally issued a public statement calling attention to the action of the lobbies. This led to a resolution in the Senate forcing all senators to expose their own business holdings which might influence their votes on the tariff. Many hearings and investigations were held, finally subduing the opposition, and the bill passed. It actually lowered the tariff below the House rates and increased the surtax on the income tax to six percent. The newspapers described the Underwood-Simmons Tariff as the first "honest" tariff since the Civil War. Through his successful fight over the bill in the Senate, Wilson's control of Congress became complete. He had also demonstrated his ability to form and lead public opinion in directions following his ideals.

In addition to the low tariff and the income tax, Wilson was now able to introduce a fundamental reform in the American banking system. The National Banking Act had become obsolete. There were no provisions for the central pooling of reserves. The check collection system on a nation-wide basis was expensive, uncertain, and involved great delay. The reserves and credit expansion capacities of the system were limited by a twenty-five percent reserve requirement. The same rigidity applied to the expansion of hand-to-hand currency, which was fixed at a maximum of somewhat over $700 million. To use the expression popular in those days, both credit and currency were "inelastic." After long and involved struggles with Congress, Wilson succeeded in getting the Federal Reserve System established.

Two other achievements of Wilson's first two years in office were the Clayton Act and Federal Trade Commission Act. According to Link, "the creation of the Federal Reserve System was the crowning achievement of the first Wilson administration." [1] But in the power struggle of the farmers and workers to wrest control of the government from business, and more particularly in the promotion of Wilson's New Freedom, the Clayton and Federal Trade Commission acts had more significance. They dealt directly with the problem of big business and the perversion and breakdown of competition. They attempted to restore some of the conditions which would prevail under pure competition.

The specific accomplishments of either the Clayton or Federal Trade Commission acts did not arouse much enthusiasm. In fact the role of Wilson in this area was severely criticized by Progressives. But the principles behind these acts contained the germ of an idea which may take root at some later period and give these acts and even Wilson's ambivalence and apparent conservatism about them great significance.

The principles of the New Freedom which were partly embodied in such legislation as the Clayton and Federal Trade Commission acts provide the philosophic basis for some of the proposals made later in this book. They supply guide lines for the restoration of a measure of freedom and individualism in a world of concentrated power. In Wilson's day these principles were neither fully appreciated nor fully understood. Public thinking had not developed far enough to accept his viewpoint or to realize its long-run significance. Because of its importance, we must at this juncture summarize the main principles of the New Freedom.

THE PRINCIPLES OF THE NEW FREEDOM

(1) The New Freedom definitely recognized that by 1912 Americans were living in a *new social order*, and that there was a social lag in our beliefs, attitudes, and laws.

(2) The new order resulted from the fact that *great corporations had become the main economic institutions* and that most men worked for them. From these facts several consequences were derived: (a) the individual had little power to control economic life; (b) his individuality was swallowed up; and (c) his relations with his employer had become impersonal. Wilson expressed it this way: "There was a time when corporations played a very minor part in our business affairs, but now they play the chief part, and most men are the servants of corporations. ... Individuality is swallowed up in the individuality and purpose of great organizations." [1]

(3) The new order is one not only where individuality is lost and corporations are dominant, but in which there is great *concentration of power*. As Wilson put it, we have a situation where "we must not pit power against weakness." [2] But he insisted that this was not so much due to the evil of men, but to the "wrongs of the system." For this reason he was reluctant to attack business or bigness as such. In the "system" the difficulties and loss of freedom were not the consequence

1 *Ibid.*, p. 5
2 *Ibid.*, p. 35

solely of what a large corporation might do to outsiders or the illegitimate privileges it exercised in the control of government. The evil was internal. It consisted also in the loss of freedom for men working *within* a corporation. Wilson was greatly concerned about this *internal* loss of freedom. In general, the Progressives looked on the outside of the large corporate structure. They were worried mainly about the power of the trusts over government from the local to the federal level.

(4) Great concentration of power caused *irresponsible and hidden use of power*. Corporations really controlled governments, not individual citizens. Therefore political power had to be returned to the people and both corporations and the government made responsible to them. As Wilson put it, "an invisible empire has been set up above the forms of democracy." [1] Wilson held this view because he believed in an organic concept of government. He could not think in terms of laws or constitutions alone. Government involved social groups. In his view, the notion that government was merely a body of laws founded on the Constitution was wrong. "The trouble with [this] theory is that government is not a machine, but a living thing. It falls, not under the [mechanical] theory of the universe, but under the theory of organic life. It is accountable to Darwin, not to Newton." [2] And in another place, he said: "By tyranny . . . we mean control of the law, of legislation and adjudication, by *organizations* [italics mine] which do not represent the people, by means which are private and selfish." [3]

(5) *The New Freedom was not opposed to bigness as such, but to monopoly, unfair competition, and the loss of freedom and opportunity for small business and the individual.* Wilson believed "Big business is to a large extent

[1] *Ibid.*, p. 35
[2] *Ibid.*, p. 47
[3] *Ibid.*, pp. 49-50

necessary and natural." [1] But trusts, he thought, were mainly based on power rather than efficiency. The small man, he believed, could defeat a trust through efficiency if he did not suffer from the unfair power exercised illegally by the trust.

(6) The New Freedom was in favor of *social justice rather than benevolence or paternalism*. Wilson did not agree with Roosevelt's attack upon the trusts, because, he claimed, Roosevelt wanted only regulation. To solve the trust problem by putting over them a regulatory commission was not enough. In the last analysis, it was the power of the trusts rather than their unfairness to which Wilson objected. Implicit in this was concern over the loss of power of the individual to do things for himself. Thus Wilson would not go along with a plan to make the trusts "good" through strong governmental regulation. To him this seemed to be a form of state benevolence or paternalism. In regard to the antitrust plank of the Progressive party, he said, "All that it complains of is—and the complaint is a just one, surely— that these gentlemen [the heads of trusts] exercise their power in a way that is secret. Therefore, we must have publicity. Sometimes they are arbitrary; therefore, they need regulation. Sometimes, they do not consult the general interests of the community; therefore, they need to be reminded of these interests by an industrial commission. But at every turn, it is the trusts who are to do us good, and *not we ourselves* [italics mine]." [2] Wilson also opposed the views of the social workers among the Progressives. They emphasized *need* rather than *justice*. To meet any social problem they favored various forms of relief to take care of needs. Wilson in addition opposed the establishment of new special privileges for farmers and workers, to offset those of big business. He wanted to abolish all special privileges.

[1] *Ibid.*, p. 164
[2] *Ibid.*, p. 195

(7) Implicit in the New Freedom philosophy are two other concepts, although these were never very fully stated. The first of these is Wilson's great and perhaps unrealistic faith in the possibility of discovering, defining, and implementing the *general interest*. He returned in his thinking to the earliest beliefs in American political theory, that government exists for the whole people and the interest of the whole can be thought of as separate from the parts. Government is not merely a compromise of all interests, a balancing of the several special interests so that a workable majority of interests may be satisfied. In the last analysis, Wilson did not believe in defining democracy as majority rule. This return to the general interest concept is of great importance and has been echoed in the utterances of Presidents Truman, Kennedy, and Johnson years later. We will have more to say about it.

(8) A second implicit concept is faith in government by law, fact-finding, and general principles, rather than by expediency and political maneuvering. Connected with this is the appearance of supposedly impartial fact-finding regulatory boards. Three of them appeared in the Wilson administration: the Federal Reserve Board, the Federal Trade Commission, and the Tariff Commission. These bodies were to act in the general interest. They were to act on the basis of facts rather than the pressures of interest groups. This action was to be based on sound economic principles. For the Federal Reserve Board, there were principles of elasticity of credit and currency and sound banking; for the Federal Trade Commission, principles of fair competition, violations of which were to be defined and prohibited; for the Tariff Commission, the concept of a scientific tariff which would account for differences in costs of production between the United States and other countries. The beginning of "egg-headism" in government is to be found in the philosophy of the New Freedom.

If government is not to be based merely upon the balancing of special interests, but on the general interest, who is to determine the general interest? Who is to determine what is best for the country as a whole? If you asked the constitutional fathers these questions, they would probably have replied that this was the work of educated men who would undertake to get all the facts and consider all sides of the questions involved. Theirs was an educated or scientific approach to government, and behind it lay the assumption of laws of nature upon which both republican and monarchical government should be based. It reflected a faith in rationality. Wilson in his *New Freedom* attempted to revive this faith in rationality, education, fact-finding, scientific laws, impartiality, and the search for the general interest.

THE LIBERALISM OF WILSON

The liberals of yesterday were more courageous than the liberals of today. La Follette, Bryan, Theodore Roosevelt and Wilson were not afraid of ideology and principles. They committed themselves to broad social viewpoints and ideals without first investigating to see whether these views would win elections. Later-day liberals have been oversensitive to the possible loss of political power. As a result, they often compromise with their principles. Although they start out as "happy warriors" they usually end as merely "happy politicians." Commitment to principle is not always good politics. One has to return to stalwarts like Wilson to find commitment to principle.

Wilson made real philosophical commitments concerning the problem of power in American life. He believed that we had evolved a new social order. The dominant institution in the new order was the great corporation. Faced with the power of the great corporation, Wilson did not jump to the easy conclusion that corporations should be regulated in order to supply the *needs* of the common or average man. He did not want to establish new privileged groups such as farmers, workers, and the unemployed alongside the managers of the large corporations in order to guarantee the satisfaction of these needs. Nevertheless, he wanted the needs of the average man to be fully met by the economy. The average man, however, should be able to satisfy his needs through his own individual efforts as a result of protection by the government of his rights to work, to do business, and to have security. Individual welfare should be sought as a *right*.

Of prime importance in Wilson's thinking were goals, methods, and theories of regulation. The New Freedom was essentially a plan for the regulation of business *in order to achieve the results of the free market* where it no longer existed. But in taking this position, Wilson committed himself simultaneously to a *goal,* a *method,* and a *theory*. The goal was the classical balance in the free market between demand and supply, which theoretically led to the lowest possible prices, to minimum profits, and to the satisfaction of the most urgent wants. The method was the solution of political and economic problems by reference to a basic principle which implemented the general interest rather than one which compromised between special interests. It was not the method of the Roosevelt-La Follette Progressives of merely satisfying needs. The theory was the price theory of classical economics.

The liberalism of Wilson was thus a principled and scientific liberalism rather than a need-oriented political liberalism. His concern for the common man did not cause him to forsake principle to meet needs. Nor did it result in mere political bargaining. He was not out to win landslide elections through promising the most to the most people. For these reasons, Wilson provided clues to the solution of our power problem. These clues consist of (1) the substitution of rights for needs, (2) the return to general interest and principled politics rather than compromised special interest politics, and (3) the foundation of national policy on scientific principles of social balance rather than on pressures of interest groups that operate without a scientific base.

V

Normalcy and The New Deal

Following Wilson in the White House was the apostle of normalcy, Warren G. Harding. He reflected the extreme reaction which had occurred, by 1920, against almost everything for which Wilson stood. In Harding's words, what the country needed was "not heroics but healing; not nostrums but normalcy; not revolution but restoration . . . not surgery but serenity." [1] In the beginning, normalcy was a vague reaction to the policies of Wilson, his idealism, and the strains of World War I. Gradually, however, it took shape in definite domestic policies and became a distinct political viewpoint.

The reaction against Wilson which produced the "return to normalcy" came from all sides. Businessmen objected to the liberals who surrounded him, to the assistance he had given organized labor, to his preachings on the need for a new social order, to the antitrust activities of his administration, to the taking over of the railroads during the war, to wartime price fixing, and to the encouragement he gave, late in his administration, to the movement for industrial democracy. Liberals, on the other hand, did not think Wilson had gone far enough. They complained that the New Freedom had been confined to the legislation of his first administration and his campaign promises in 1916. They were angered by

[1] Beard, *op. cit.*, p. 664

the restrictions on socialists and radicals imposed by Post-master Burleson. Labor and farm groups also complained that Wilson had not aided them sufficiently. There was, of course, the reaction against the League of Nations, the desire to return to isolationism, the growing cynicism about the causes and purposes of the war. It was a war to protect American rights on the high seas, not to make the world safe for democracy. But most important, it was argued that Wilson had never had a popular mandate for his policies. When elected in 1912, he was short by two million votes of a clear majority. His reelection in 1916 was due to the peculiar circumstances created by the war. Business men were convinced that the public had never really turned against business and its control of the Federal Government.

They were convinced also that the country had had a narrow escape. Wilson's unsound economic policies, they thought, had created the depression of 1913, and this depression might have continued and become more severe had it not been for the economic stimulation provided by World War I. As a result, the country was saved by the war from the "bitter fruits of fanaticism." [1] There was a need to rescind the unwise legislation, restore businessmen to power in Washington, and return to the policies of Hamilton, Clay, Webster, and McKinley. From a domestic policy standpoint, this was what normalcy meant to businessmen.

THE NATURE OF NORMALCY AND ITS OPPONENTS

When the voters overwhelmingly elected Harding instead of Governor Cox, Harding undertook to introduce the program of normalcy, the concrete expression of which involved (1) a return to a high tariff, (2) the reduction of the surtax rates on the income and estate taxes, (3) the repeal of the gift tax, (4) the reduction of suits against business under the antitrust laws, (5) opposition to the soldiers' bonus, (6) op-

[1] Beard, *op. cit.,* p. 668

position to protective labor legislation, (7) opposition to farm price and subsidy legislation, and (8) the lease of valuable parts of the public domain—making clear that businessmen were to be restored to influence in Washington.

Harding was not very successful in restoring normalcy in terms of the above eight points except that a high tariff was adopted through the Fordney-McCumber Act. He died in office in a cloud of scandal connected with Teapot Dome, and to Coolidge was left the task of fully establishing normalcy. There were reasons for Harding's failure. Although big business again controlled the Presidency, it did not yet control Congress. Liberal and farm-oriented congressmen blocked the reduction of progressive taxation and the elimination of measures supporting the farmers. The progressive movement was weak but not dead. Progressivism persisted under the leadership of Robert La Follette and stemmed from two sources, the Nonpartisan League and the Farm Bureau Federation.

CALVIN COOLIDGE

By 1924, Coolidge and the Republicans had gained headway in convincing the public of the need for normalcy, and the farmer and labor organizations had lost ground. Not the least factor in this political trend was the growing postwar prosperity. By 1929, Coolidge and Hoover had achieved the full normalcy program: taxes had been reduced, the gift tax was repealed, and business was firmly in control of the Federal Government. The policy of laissez-faire had been reestablished. The farm subsidy proposals had been defeated.

By the time of Coolidge's administration, the liberal struggle for power had weakened to the point where it seemed utterly and hopelessly dead, never to be resurrected. The vast majority of the voters had been convinced of the following views: (1) It was unwise to challenge the control of the Federal Government by business. (2) The evils of monopoly had been successfully attacked and removed by the trust-busting of Theodore Roosevelt and no further curbs were needed. (3) The control of business by government was unwise and likely to destroy prosperity. (4) The control of government by business would promote efficient government and create prosperity. (5) The prosperity of business would trickle down to the general public and make everyone prosperous. (6) The best economic policies for the government to pursue were those of the Hamilton-McKinley tradition. (7) The common man was rapidly becoming an owner of business himself through the widespread purchase of stock. (8) Soon there would be no distinction between labor and capital.

Let us quote from Coolidge to express the temper of the times. "What we need is thrift and industry.... Let everybody keep at work.... We have come to our present high estate through toil and suffering and sacrifice.... Not by revolution but by evolution has man worked out his destiny.... We are all members of one body.... Industry cannot flourish if labor languishes.... Transportation cannot prosper if manufactures decline.... Large profits mean large payrolls.... McKinley was the advance agent of prosperity that he might be the prophet of the intellectual and moral forces of mankind." [1]

Although the spirit of normalcy captured the thinking of the vast majority of city dwellers, the farmers during this period remained restive. The prosperity which spread to the rest of the nation in the period after 1924 did not come to them. Agricultural prices fell sharply after 1920 and reached a low level. They got out of line more and more with industrial prices, and farm debts mounted. There was a declining market for farm products abroad. The farmer found himself waiting for a prosperity that did not come; and farm price theorists evolved the concept of parity, an

[1] Beard, *op. cit.*, vol. 2, pp. 700-701

equation of farm and industrial prices to be established by government action raising farm prices. The farmer quietly lost his faith in the laissez-faire which was the watchword of the rest of the nation.

Unrest developed in this period in other quarters. It was one of hard sledding for labor unions, whose membership fell from over 4,000,000 in 1920 to 1,500,000 in 1929. Labor had not won exemption from attack under the antitrust laws, and the Republican administrations were vigorously anti-labor. The right of collective bargaining was not accepted; secondary boycotts and strikes were illegal. Employers conducted anti-union campaigns, combatting labor through labor spies, company unions, pension systems, and welfare programs. But the main cause of union weakness was probably the growing white-collar character of labor. Most workers did not want to be in the working class. They were convinced of the identity of their interests with those of large corporations and employers. In some parts of labor, fear played a role also. With union activity a basis for firing, only the courageous wished to run the risks of such activity.

THE DEPRESSION OF 1929

The revival of the American power problem and its present form and significance may be traced to the 1929 depression. The period of serenity and normalcy ended in an economic debacle. The severity of this depression amounted to a national catastrophe and came close to overturning the capitalist system. We know now that many maladjustments from 1922 to 1929 prepared the way for the collapse, but such was the state of economic knowledge and forecasting in those years that the depression came to many as a surprise.

Among the maladjustments that were present in the twenties were the following:

(1) International trade and financial relations were out of balance. A high tariff prevented extensive imports and

the United States continued an export surplus, lending money to foreigners so that they could pay for our imports. Ultimately these debts could not be paid and the export surplus and credit structure on which they were based collapsed simultaneously.

(2) The recovery of European agriculture after the war and the great increase in farm productivity in our own nation led to a sick farm economy, suffering from a growing disparity between farm and industrial prices. Farm purchasing power, on which the rest of the economy partly depended, fell from year to year.

(3) The great growth of industrial productivity was not accompanied by a rise in consumer income sufficiently rapid to keep pace with its growth. The remedy of installment selling appeared, but, in the end, this did not grow fast enough to meet the need for increased purchasing power. Instead, we began to have an increase in technological and long-run unemployment.

Whatever the antecedents of the depression, it resulted in unemployment at maximum in the neighborhood of 14,000,000 persons and created need and insecurity at almost all levels of society. It brought with it the election of Franklin D. Roosevelt and the era known as the New Deal. Although the New Deal sought mainly to provide relief and promote recovery, the manner in which it attempted to accomplish these purposes created and employed new alignments of power in American society. It is with these alignments and the theory of power underlying them that we are here concerned. But in order to delineate these new lines of power in a realistic way, we must describe some of the history of the New Deal.

THE NEW DEAL

The New Deal was a frantic and enormous experimental program which changed from year to year. It was not planned, nor was it based on any given theory of politics or school of economic thought. One thing can be said with certainty: all New Dealers opposed laissez-faire and were fond of referring to laissez-faire as "dead." From 1933 to the present time the Federal Government has been strongly interventionist.

Along with the abandonment of laissez-faire came the rejection of other beliefs common in the normalcy period. For example, it was no longer believed that the control of government by business would insure prosperity. On the contrary, the wisdom of this control was challenged by the vast majority of the voters. Many of these blamed the depression on the business policy-makers and some on the capitalist system itself. Although Wilson may not have had a clear mandate to restore the Federal Government to the general public, Roosevelt certainly did.

The depression also caused a sharp decline in faith in individual responsibility. In its place came a new belief in social responsibility. To the end of his administration, Hoover had insisted that the Federal Government was not responsible for either recovery or relief. The public now insisted that it was. In addition, the "trickle down" theory was abandoned. The New Deal soon turned away from aid to business as the exclusive means of bringing about recovery and put most of its effort into direct aid to the unemployed and to the destitute farmers. Belief that the common man was in partnership with business or shared business interests was vigorously challenged. Finally, faith in classical economics and in the laws of supply and demand, which supposedly would automatically bring about recovery and full employment, vanished completely. Although the New Dealers were not devoted to any one new school of economics, they were opposed to the basic tenets of the old classicism.

When Roosevelt assumed the Presidency in March, 1933, the country had reached a low point. The banks were closing and there was a run on most of them for the conversion of paper money into gold. His first task was to restore order in banking by ending the convertibility of paper money. Once this emergency had been met, he and his Congress could turn to the three great aspects of the New Deal—Relief, Recovery, and Reform. The most urgent of these was relief.

RELIEF

The New Deal became a labyrinth of alphabetical agencies. In the field of relief, the first of these was FERA, the Federal Emergency Relief Administration, which lasted from 1933 to 1935, when the WPA, or Works Progress Administration, took its place. The FERA abandoned the Hoover philosophy that relief should be the responsibility of private charitable organizations or of local governments. There was no alternative to federal relief. Private agencies in ordinary times had been dispensing charity at the rate of only $1,000,000 a month, but by the winter of 1932 they were called upon for $10 million a month. Soon the local governments, as well as private agencies, had relief loads that they could not carry. The states entered the relief picture because they had greater borrowing and taxing power. But by 1933, the burden had proved too great even for the states. In the three years of its operation, the FERA was to spend $4,353 million, or about $121 million a month.

The FERA granted money to state emergency relief agencies, to be used by the states to provide direct relief on the basis of *need*. Altogether, the Federal Government financed approximately seventy percent of the total cost of relief in those years, and the states and localities the remainder. By 1935, strong opposition had developed to the FERA, which was called the "dole." Our American individualism reacted against granting money solely in terms of need. It was also charged that the relief system was encouraging people to remain unemployed, and that the distribution of relief funds was not strictly according to need, or, inversely, according to the ability of the states to pay, but was determined by political opportunism.[1]

The FERA reflected the spirit of the New Deal and the forces that went into it in the beginning. Roosevelt gathered around him men of good will who were not overly concerned with theories or standards. They had two objectives in mind: immediate relief to the impoverished, and the promotion of recovery. Social workers exercised a powerful influence in the early days, and Harry Hopkins remained one of Roosevelt's principal advisers through the subsequent war period. It will be remembered that social workers strongly influenced the progressive movement, but since this movement never succeeded in gaining power, what liberals and social workers wanted was never fully achieved in Washington. In the Roosevelt administration, the social workers finally triumphed. They exalted need as a motivating force and they relegated theory to the background. They were perhaps the principal determiners of policy in the early New Deal, 1933-1935. The social workers and unorthodox economists from whom Roosevelt took advice were the brain trust of the early New Deal. Behind them, and giving them enormous power, were the unemployed, most of the farmers, organized liberals, the southern Democrats, and the middle and lower classes of the country. The political alignment of farmers and workers, which developed in Bryan's day and almost crystallized in 1916 under Wilson, now appeared complete and in tremendous force as a result of the depression. It can be called the *Grand Alliance*. It stood for swift government intervention, but had no clear theoretical orientation.

The WPA and the PWA (Public Works Administration), which followed the early relief program, were inconsistent in some respects with this power drive of farmers, workers, and the lower middle class. The work relief program of WPA

[1] *Cf.* Withers, W., *Financing Economic Security*, Ch. 3-4

was in part a reaction in favor of the individualism latent in American thinking. A person should have a job, even if that job is created for him. He should not receive something for nothing. What he received should also be varied according to the extent of his productivity. Under the WPA, only the employable population were to receive relief, and this meant that about half of those on relief (the so-called unemployables) were turned over to the states for care without the benefit of the federal grants of funds which had been available under the FERA. It was the beginning of the decline of the "need," "social work," or "progressive" approach to the problems of the crisis. At the time, the nature of this change was not fully understood by the New Dealers, who were merely reacting to adverse criticism.

The New Deal shifted from need to price control as the basic of relief with the passage of the Agricultural Adjustment Act and the administration it created. It was thought that a surplus of farm products resulted in a price level at which the farmer could not produce except at a loss. Under the provisions of the act, acreage was cut down through contracts with farmers, and, in return, they received a government subsidy. The funds for these crop restriction payments were obtained from the proceeds of the agricultural processing taxes levied on grain mills and other processors. The extent of the restriction decided upon was determined by an amount which would supposedly raise the price of the product to "parity." In the beginning, parity meant the prices that prevailed between 1909 and 1914. In these years, which were prosperous ones for the farmers, agricultural prices were supposedly on a par with industrial prices. Thus parity meant bringing farm prices up to the level of industrial prices, a level from which they had sunk since 1909-1914. The main theoretical purposes behind the Agricultural Adjustment Act, however, were to destroy competition and to create monopoly in farming. The parity concept was merely a justification of these main purposes.

Both the relief acts and the AAA would have been regarded as expressions of progressivism. They were special privilege measures—one to aid mainly the unemployed city workers, the other to aid the farmers. They were measures that represented benevolent state paternalism. They had no basis in right or individual responsibility.

RECOVERY

A more comprehensive phase of New Dealism was introduced by the National Industrial Recovery Act of 1933. At the time, there was much mention of cutthroat or wasteful competition. The Recovery Act undertook to eliminate this through the enactment of codes of "fair competition." Each industry, through its trade association, was to draw up a code consisting of provisions for production quotas, prices, and business practices that would promote fair competition. The codes were then to be submitted to the code authority for review. Hearings were held, presumably to see to it that the interests of industry, labor, the consumer, and the public in general were protected. Once a code was accepted by the National Recovery Administration, it was signed by the President and became the law of the industry. Infractions could be punished by a fine of $500 for each violation. Although the codes had many provisions, the most important were those which raised prices and reduced output. The purpose was to create monopoly where it had not existed before. Monopoly was legalized, and the NIRA was a complete about-face from the antitrust and unfair competition legislations of 1890 and 1914. Through monopoly power, prices could be raised above costs. Reasonable profits would be restored and price cutting ended. The increase in profits supposedly would bring about recovery and increase employment.

But the actual effects of the NIRA were both disastrous and futile. By 1934, industrial output had declined and unemployment began to increase. Prices rose faster than purchasing power, causing a decline in demand, production, and employment. In many fields the codes were unenforceable. Although Hugh Johnson, the administrator of the act, made many threats to "crack down" on code violators, the violations became too numerous to be dealt with. The competitive spirit was great in depressed times. By shading the code prices, more business could be done. Long before the law was declared unconstitutional in the Schecter Case, the breakdown in enforcement had nullified many of the codes. In short, the effort to give monopoly power to small as well as large business had failed.

The relief programs of the New Deal demonstrated a growing emphasis on meeting need. This was a throwback to the progressive movement of 1910-1912. The AAA and NIRA represented the regulation of the economic system for the welfare of the underprivileged groups, farmers, and small business men, an approach which also resembled the thinking of the Progressives. But there was something new here. *It was belief in achieving economic balance by universalizing monopoly* and by granting monopoly power to the underprivileged. This policy did not actually bring recovery; in fact, it hindered it. But at the time there were many who believed that recovery could be achieved through these methods.

The same type of thinking pervaded the labor policies of the New Deal. In the NIRA there were a number of labor provisions. First, the codes themselves were to provide for higher wages and shorter hours. Higher wages, like higher prices, were thought to provide higher purchasing power. There was confusion here between higher wages and higher general purchasing power. Higher wages would provide higher purchasing power granted the same level of employment. But unemployment increased during the NIRA period.

In addition to higher-wage provisions, the NIRA contained the famous Section 7a, which established the right of collective bargaining. As was intended, the organization of labor began to increase rapidly under the protection of the law. Over 700,000 new members were added to the ranks of organized labor before the NIRA was declared unconstitutional in 1935. After the Supreme Court ruling, Congress enacted the National Labor Relations Act of 1935 (the Wagner Act) which reestablished the right of collective bargaining.

Before the New Deal, organized labor was a relatively weak force in the nation. Large areas of labor—such as steel, rubber, automobile and aircraft workers—were only thinly organized. Union organization was strong only in the clothing trades, mining, the railroads, and the building trades. As a result of the New Deal legislation, industrial fields began to be organized. This trend was hastened by the Committee on Industrial Organization, which attempted to organize labor in industries instead of by trade or craft. Ultimately it became a national federation of industrial unions separate from the American Federation of Labor. When the great wave of labor organization had largely run its course, the total number in unions had reached 15,000,000, or about one quarter of all workers. White-collar workers and many other large groups, however, remained outside the unions. Nevertheless, unions have become a very powerful force in the economy, because the fields organized are essential to the functioning of the economy—mining, transportation, steel, automobile, and aircraft.

From the standpoint of the political balance of power, the organization of labor with the aid of New Deal legislation was most significant. Political power is based largely on external economic organization. Not only did farmers and workers join together in 1932 to oust business from the control of the Federal Government; they were themselves

strengthened in terms of both income and external organization by the government they had elected. In the administration of the government in Washington, the economist, social
worker, labor leader, and farmer crowded out the business
or civil service executive of earlier days. There was a new
orientation of political power, corresponding more closely
than before to the numbers of voters; and this new orientation was largely maintained until the approach of World
War II. No wonder that the conservative wing of business
so bitterly attacked the New Deal. Some liberal businessmen
played their part in the program, and large sectors of business
profited from the recovery that was achieved, but it was disturbing to see the government run by and for non-business-
men. Perhaps this was more disturbing to business than the
unorthodox theories and policies of the New Dealers.

Insofar as the New Deal brought recovery from one of the
worst depressions the country ever suffered, it did so through
what is popularly known as *deficit spending*. From 1933 to
1937, the budget of the Federal Government ran a deficit.
Again in 1939 deficits appeared. Heavy deficits continued
throughout World War II. The federal debt increased from
$16 billion in 1932 to $41 billion in 1939. By the end of the
war, it had reached $272 billion. During the New Deal years,
the average deficit was $3 to $4 billion a year. At its peak, the
war caused a deficit of $50 billion in one year. As the debt
mounted from the deficits, we recovered substantially from
the 1929 depression and went on after the war to full employment and a prosperity in which real income rose by fifty
percent.

REFORM

The New Deal attempted to make fundamental social and
economic reforms. Among the reform laws passed were the
Social Security Act and the Securities and Securities Exchange
acts. By far the most significant was the Social Security Act.

This comprehensive measure resulted in the establishment of systems of unemployment insurance in all states, noncontributory payments to the aged and other groups in need, and contributory insurance for the aged and their survivors, financed by payroll taxes on employers and employees. Social insurance protection was established as a right.

In summary, the depression and the New Deal program meant fundamental changes in the American power structure.

(1) The depression brought the problem of power acutely into the open again.

(2) The New Deal took over a government which had been controlled by business, especially big business, at a time when farmers, workers, home owners, the aged, and small businessmen were suffering hardship and were without power.

(3) The New Deal shifted government power to a coalition of these groups, the *Grand Alliance*.

(4) The New Deal helped to organize some of these groups externally, with the result that their political and economic power grew and became concentrated and monopolistic.

In bringing about these changes, a new conflict over political and economic power was created by Roosevelt. The consequences of the New Deal were humanitarian, but they caused a serious impasse in American economic life and led to a further destruction of individualism, both politically and economically. Wendell Willkie sought to reverse these trends in 1940. But Roosevelt triumphed and firmly established a new political era in which huge new power groups subordinated the individual and competed seriously with large corporations which had already diminished individualism. Not only laissez-faire, but most of our economic and political individualism was now dead.

The effect of the New Deal in creating new power groups and power drives, which along with the concentration of power in the hands of big businesses threaten individualism and democracy, has not been fully understood. Even those who urged a return to laissez-faire were not fully cognizant of the real nature of the power changes caused by New Dealism. Corporate concentration and dynamic materialism had gone far toward destroying individualism and democracy even before 1932. The New Deal completed the job, although seeking to aid the common man through a program of relief, recovery, and reform essentially based on *need* rather than on *individual rights* or *justice*.

THE LIBERALISM OF FRANKLIN ROOSEVELT

Perhaps the significance of Franklin Roosevelt and the New Dealism he introduced will be subject to controversial interpretations no matter how much perspective we get from the passage of time. But probably no one will deny that Roosevelt's approach to social problems was vastly different from that of Wilson. Roosevelt and the people who influenced him were pragmatic and politically oriented. They followed in many ways the methods of the Progressives. Need and want were paramount and urgent, and they had no time to bother with principles or involved intellectualism. This is understandable in view of the catastrophic depression with which they had to cope.

But a liberalism which bases its efforts on meeting need and subordinates principles is dangerous in a power-structured society. It leads to the political organization of powerful competing groups and relegates the individual and his rights to the background. To "get anywhere" one must be a member of a group in a manner which is essentially political. Moreover, the needs which are satisfied are likely to vary inversely with the political pressure one's group can exert, and have no connection with the general interest. In addition, needs and goals become all-important, and means are relegated to the background. The Rooseveltian type of leadership came dangerously near the position that the ends justify the means.

Most serious, however, was the development of competing organized power groups and the personal appeal to these groups to crush opposition. Rooseveltian leadership followed some of the tactics of totalitarianism. Leadership was by personality and slogan. Emotional loyalty was deeply aroused. Wide-scale organization was the main tool of power. Of course, there were vast differences as to the ends sought, the subordination of individuals involved, and the degree of irrationality. But the pragmatic, personality, power-group leadership of the New Deal was closer in method to totalitarianism than it was to the approach of Wilson or even of Truman.

Roosevelt returned to the unintellectualism of the Progressives and social workers. This may seem strange in view of the brain trust of the New Deal. Although the brain trust provided numerous and conflicting ideas and gave the New Deal academic prestige, it provided no ideology as a basis for policy. It did not seek to establish policy on the firm foundation of a new body of social science which would replace classicism and rationalize the new power-structured society. This failure was due to Roosevelt himself, whose leadership was basically unintellectual though profoundly humanitarian.

In a sense, the Rooseveltian liberalism was a transitional phenomenon. The common man had lost power. He had to be organized to regain power in competition with the power of the great corporation. He suffered from urgent and acute economic needs during and after the Great Depression. These needs had to be met and economic recovery promoted. This was accomplished by organization and a great change in the balance of political and economic power. But once the ends were largely accomplished and a new power structure created, there were no guide lines for future social policy. The old balance of power and the old classical ideology of the free market and laissez-faire had been destroyed. But what new method of preventing power conflicts, maintaining a balance of power, and protecting the general interest and welfare of the common man was provided? Roosevelt created a bridge from the old to the new, but never really got us firmly across that bridge.

The failure can be excused in view of the manifold problems he faced—too many for the lifetime of one leader, no matter how great. But it cannot be excused in present-day liberal leadership, which continues to follow a non-ideological personality approach. We need to return to the Wilsonian approach of basing leadership on scientific thought.

LACK OF ECONOMIC UNDERSTANDING

During the depression of 1929 and the years between the depression and World War II, a tremendous lag appeared in popular understanding of economic and political problems. Even the old classical economics which Hoover invoked as the basis of recovery from the depression was understood by the general public only on terms of a few almost meaningless clichés such as "supply equals demand," or "competition is the life of trade." Economics was taught to only a very small part of the population, mostly on the college level, and then in such a boring and unrealistic way that it was promptly forgotten by many students. There was little historical perspective and few understood the great economic changes that had taken place since the Civil War, or the new forms of economics which were developing. Judging from the newspaper and magazine articles and the speeches made in Congress and in political gatherings, people were better informed about economic issues between 1890 and 1916 than they were between 1920 and 1929. We had gone backwards, and our lack of understanding in the thirties persists to the present day.

The development of Goldwaterism and the degeneration of the Presidential campaign in 1964 into a discussion of personality problems and scandal reveals a lack of interest in basic issues as well as a critical lack of understanding. Perhaps the Rooseveltian type of liberal leadership was caused partly by the ignorance and lack of interest of the general public in economic and social theory. Perhaps ignorance partly explains the persistence of this type of leadership. But our confusion over the power problem in the United States grows out of a lack of understanding. If we are ever to solve the power problem, we need greater knowledge of basic economic theory and a leadership that relies on this knowledge. One insight to be gained from our survey of the history of the problem is the need for an intellectual approach. We need new socioeconomic theory which can become the basis of a new ideology and a related group of policies. But to reach this point, we must first postulate new theory which liberal leaders and the general public will accept. We will begin an attempt to do this in the succeeding chapter.

VI

Classical Economics and the Power Problem

A s WE have stated in the last chapter, our failure to understand the effects of materialism and concentrated corporate,
union, and political power in destroying American individualism and democracy is due in no small measure to our
ignorance concerning economic and social principles. Although economic thought explaining and analyzing the
trends away from individualism developed early in our national life, it failed to grow into a full body of economic and
political principles which justified in theory the new social
and economic structure which was developing. Smith in
economics and Locke and Montesquieu in political theory
had rationalized the eighteenth and early nineteenth century individualistic money economy with its emphasis on
small farms and small businesses. Although most American
intellectuals first followed the Physiocrats, classical doctrines
were exported to the United States and the rest of the world
and came to be the accepted orthodoxy. In democratic
countries, however, as economic life became industrialized
and concentrated, a new body of theory arose that undertook
to rationalize these conditions, but only in a fragmentary
way. The little that appeared failed to achieve wide acceptance, and was never able to challenge seriously the older
individualistic theory.

It can be said without dispute that Marxism was the only comprehensive theoretical structure which really competed with classical economics and classical political science in the nineteenth century. But despite the fact that it challenged the older faith in individualism, it never made us question the degree to which we were actually democratic. It provoked doubt only as to the future of capitalism and its ability to raise the standard of living of the working classes. Thus, prior to the communist philosophy of Lenin, Marxism was revolutionary as to capitalism but not as to democracy. It was even regarded as democratic, in that it favored the masses and preached equality of wealth. The dictatorship of the proletariat postulated in the Communist Manifesto was regarded as a temporary moratorium on democratic government, not as a permanent substitute for it.

It is necessary to realize that an economic rationale for a hierarchical power-structured society, or even for a moderately industrialized and monopolized society, would have had to challenge our democratic principles. To do this in the nineteenth century would have seemed more revolutionary than Marxism. So long as our economic system remained competitive and small-scale, it could be equalitarian and individualistic. This was democratic and morally right. Could we say that monopoly and bigness which were not equalitarian and which subordinated the individual were right? Not unless we abandoned our faith in individualism and democracy. As big business and monopoly grew, we had two alternatives. We could regard them as bad, or we could indulge in inconsistency. In America, some followed the first course. They fought monopoly. Others regarded bigness and monopoly as good, secretly or openly, but refused to see any inconsistency between a power society and democratic government or individualism. Had these latter people or their economic rationalizers boldly challenged democracy in favor of bigness or power, or rationalized as to the consistency of bigness and democracy, our thinking about democracy would probably not now be so confused. The threat of power to democracy would have been openly discussed and the alternatives fully considered.

Classical economics, as we have seen, remained as the orthodox explanation and justification of American economic life until men's thinking about economic matters was rudely shaken by the catastrophic depression of 1929. According to classical theory, the economic system was governed by the laws of supply and demand, these operating to bring about balance through price changes. If the supply of goods or labor became too great for the demand, prices or wages had to fall until demand again equalled supply. Shortages would cause the opposite results. A shortage of workers would lead to higher wages; a shortage of meat to a higher price for meat. As prices fell, producers in the field would leave it to go into other fields where prices and profits were higher. Workers would shift to fields where they could get more employment or higher wages. Assuming free market prices, perfect competition, and the mobility of labor, capital, and resources, there could be no overproduction, no underproduction, and no depressions.

Unfortunately, because of the great decline in competition and economic mobility by 1929, the depression did not automatically correct itself through the action of the laws of supply and demand. Labor and capital remained unemployed, and the unemployment got worse. Consequently, President Hoover and the Republicans who supported him were thrown out of office. They believed in laissez-faire. They thought that no government action was needed to bring recovery. The free price system would ultimately restore balance. After waiting for this to happen during more than two years of very acute suffering, the American people lost faith in classical doctrine and in the President who believed in it.

However, although faith was lost in classicism as a basis

for economic recovery policies, the American people continued to regard classical theory as an ideal body of economic morals. *The classical principles were no longer right, but righteous.* The human mind is capable of a vast amount of compartmentalization. We can separate our moral life from our real life. This is especially true when we are unable or afraid to make the two consistent. Although largely discarding the economics of the classicists as a guide to practical governmental policy, many Americans could still adhere to the ideals or morals of classicism. They did not want to become immoral by deserting their old morals without finding a new body of morals to substitute. *And no one really provided a substitute.* As we have said, early in the nineteenth century abortive attempts were made to develop a new American economics and new economic morals. But the early efforts in this direction by men like Daniel Raymond and Henry Carey failed.

As we have said previously, we need a new social economics suited to an age of centralized power. But, in society, we can never begin something new without referring to the past. More than this, what is new is never, in the end, completely new. It consists of a synthesis of the new and the old. Society is a chain of continuous development, and revolutions are not absolute breaks in the chain, but periods of acceleration in the synthesis of the new and the old. Our point of departure for a new socioeconomic concept therefore must be the classicism from which most American thinking stems. Moreover, classicism was the essence of individualism, and if we are somehow to restore individualism and democracy in a concentrated economic world, we must reexamine the early fundamental arrangements in classical economics which once made it possible. What, then, were the basic tenets of classicism?

CLASSICAL ECONOMICS AND THE POWER PROBLEM

The classical economists did not arrive at their generalizations about the economic system through inductive methods. To use modern terminology, they established a "model" of an ideal economic system based upon the assumptions of free competition, mobility, and rationality. To some extent some parts of our economic life have conformed to the classical model. But classical economics has always been more of an economic ideal than an explanation. To many, the programs of the Progressives and the later New Dealers were not objectionable because they violated classical laws of economic truth, but because they denied the classical morals and ideals. Even today, this is what mainly worries conservatives about the progressive policies of the Federal Government.

THE IDEAL CLASSICAL MODEL

The classical ideals, however, are inseparable from the classical description of how a free economy works. Let us review in outline form the classical economic model.

(1) *Supply creates demand.* Because a person produces a saleable, or demanded, commodity or service, he is able to demand other commodities or services in exchange for what he has produced. This concept is often referred to as *Say's Law.*

(2) If supply creates demand, there will be *no overproduction or underproduction* and *no unemployment,* provided there is a free market price system. If a man produces something and cannot sell all of it at a given price, he will reduce the price until he can sell it.

(3) *Demand equals supply* in a free competitive market system. This point is really the explanation of the preceding point. Sellers of goods, labor, and capital offer these economic supplies to buyers. As the offering price falls, the

demand increases. This is the so-called *law of demand*, that demand varies inversely with price. As higher prices are offered by buyers, the suppliers offer more. This is the opposite, or *law of supply*, that supply varies directly with price. The classicists visualized ideal free markets in which buyers offered higher prices and sellers lower prices until balance was reached with demand equaling supply. This was called the *equilibrium* price, and the concept may be referred to as *classical equilibrium*.

(4) Another tenet of classicism was that prices equal the cost of production at the "margin." Producers were assumed to have different degrees of efficiency, and they would produce more goods as long as the price in the market was higher or at least equal to their costs plus a minimum profit.

The implication of this classical principle is that, granted free markets, the inefficient are driven out or turn to fields where they can be efficient. The result of the free market is thus to shift capital and labor to the fields where they are most efficient, i.e., to produce *maximum efficiency*. Thus competition is desirable because it causes efficiency.

Related to this more formal economic analysis were the three basic norms or criteria of classicism. They were (1) that free prices and free markets are the guides to economic activity and the only desirable guides; (2) that free competition is the "life of trade" and essential to the efficient functioning of free markets; and (3) that any interference with free markets by government or monopoly (conspiracies in restraint of trade) destroys the efficiency of the economic system. The last of these three criteria is, of course, the doctrine of *laissez-faire*.

It is easy to regard classicism as merely a body of economic theories designed to show how the economic system can be most efficiently organized and how it can be balanced and kept in perfect equilibrium. However, as the early classicists well knew, it was much more than a body of economic theory. It was a doctrine of political economy, or of the relation of government to economic life. To the classicist, economics and government were inseparable. Economics was, indeed, a form of economic government where individuals were governed by natural laws and where there was majority rule. The individual acted by himself, or, as they were fond of saying, "in his own self-interest." He was not restrained by men, but only by the natural laws of supply, demand, and cost. There was no dictatorship or absolute monarchy in the economic world. There was, instead, free competition and laissez-faire. The role of political government was confined to the protection of property and the maintenance of the "rules of the game." It could not compete with or replace private enterprise. It could not even regulate it, except insofar as it regulated to maintain free and honest markets. Nor could groups of men other than the government conspire to reduce or eliminate the free action of the market. Any restraint of trade, whether publicly or privately inspired, was contrary to the basic individualistic philosophy of classical economists.

THE CLASSICAL WORLD OF NO POWER

At this point, we can begin to see the relationship to the power problem of classical economics and the hypothetical economic and political world which it postulated. The classical world was one of "no power." No individual had great, or, in fact, any power over any other individual. Since the state was forbidden to interfere with individuals through its power and since economic power groups were also forbidden, there was no power situation of any sort, and also *no power problem.* In the economic world, men acted individually, with no one man having much more economic strength than any other. Few, if any, could force others to do their bidding, and, correspondingly, few were seriously dependent upon others for their livelihood.

It must be remembered that this is not the real but the idealistic picture of classical economic life in the nineteenth and early twentieth centuries. While the economists were describing and preaching this ideal system, employers were acquiring more and more power over workers. Producers were acquiring increasing power over consumers. Monopolies and restraints of trade created small islands of economic power in many parts of the economy. Government itself was becoming slowly but definitely more regulatory. Great fortunes were developed by the more successful business families, creating power from the mere differences in wealth themselves. People and their compliance could be bought. All this the classical economists were happy to ignore as exceptions to the general rule. Some who did not ignore it inveighed morally against it. But they were reformers. They remained true to the system of free capitalism as the best of all possible worlds. They did not abandon it like the Marxists or imagine that a new social order was developing that called for new explanations and a new politico-economic concept.

Having pointed out the growing contradictions of reality with theory, it must be said in defense of classicism that it did describe a large part of the real world of the nineteenth century. No other system of thought either described or explained it as well. No system of thought ever achieves the importance and acceptance of Smith's *Wealth of Nations* without having strong roots in reality. A great shift had occurred in the character of economic life from 1300, when feudalism began to decline, to be replaced by increasing statism and finally by a large measure of individualism and free enterprise. Classicism purported to describe and defend this final stage in the evolution and, as such, it was viable. The difficulty with classicism as carried over into the twentieth century was that it described and justified an economic system which no longer existed in large and important segments of the total economy.

Despite the fact that in the first half of the nineteenth century classical economics and its related ethics suited large parts of the real economic world, this ceased to be true in the twentieth century. The decline of competition, the growth of large-scale industrialism, the dominance of the large corporation, the power of advertising, and the decrease in economic mobility made classicism largely inapplicable. Its economics, at least, was no longer valid. Instead of a world of "no power," we lived in a world of power.

The farmers and liberals in the progressive movement, as we have seen in a previous chapter, were the first to realize that *the introduction of bigness had created a power problem.* In their opinion, it was not merely monopoly, but bigness itself, which created the problem. But could the free enterprise system be restored by "trust-busting"? Roosevelt and Wilson thought not. But if the free enterprise system could not be restored, was regulation of bigness the answer to this immoral situation? And if regulation was the answer, for what goals should the regulation be undertaken? These questions plagued Wilson especially, because he adhered to classical principles.

CLASSICAL PHILOSOPHY AND THE POWER PROBLEM

Having reached the position that monopoly and concentration of power are destructive of freedom, it might easily be concluded, as it was by the Progressives, that regulation of big business in the interest of the public and public relief on the basis of need were the answers. But no one affected by classicism could be satisfied with such answers. Justice, not benevolence, was what Wilson wanted. The common man, he said, needs a chance to earn what is due him, not charity. Thus the mere regulation of business in the interest of the general public and public relief measures might meet unsatisfied *needs,* but they would not restore *freedom* and *justice.*

The effect of classicism upon liberals like Wilson was to cause them to *search for more than the satisfaction of need*. One might say that three points are involved here: need, means, and goals. The progressive, like the social worker, saw the plight of the farmer, the evils of child labor, the injustice of long hours of labor, the tyranny of big business. Changes were required to remove privilege and meet needs. Government had to regulate big business and provide relief to effect these changes. But the regulation was a method that in itself destroyed the freedoms of the economic system. Moreover, unless the government was to meet need by helping the individual to meet his needs by himself, freedom and individualism were being abandoned. Finally, if the government was to take over the task of meeting needs, what were the "true" needs? To what ends should government regulation be directed? Should new privileges be established for farmers and workers, to replace or match the privileges of big business? The significance of classical economics lies in the approach that it suggests for the power problem. One affected by classicism cannot merely propose the strong regulation of business by government.

CLASSICISM AS A REGULATORY MODEL

Since no realistic person can think in terms of actually recreating a free competitive economic system corresponding to the classical economic model, classicism, if it is to be followed at all, has to become an ideal or goal upon which the regulation of business can be based. If one views classicism in terms of a goal or an ideal, what can it mean? The answer lies in a return to the classical principles stated above and to the basic tenets of classical economics. What classical economics sought was an efficient, equalitarian, free, and well-balanced economy. *Efficiency, equality, freedom, and balance* were the goals. Excessive concentration of economic power could conceivably have an adverse effect on all four goals.

To illustrate, let us think of an all-powerful monopolistic large corporation. Without the check of competition, there would be less inducement to efficiency than under free enterprise. To be sure, the profit motive would still operate to promote efficiency, but not in the rigorous way in which the competitive threat to survival disciplines business in nonmonopolistic spheres. Both internally and externally, quality would be lost. No small competitor, however efficient, could hope to succeed. Moreover, the individual within the huge hierarchy of the corporation would have far less freedom than would be the case in a small corporation. Last, economic balance in the classical sense would be lost.

Since the free market creates those degrees and kinds of relationships between prices, wages, and other costs which lead to efficiency and balance, the regulation of business should also seek these goals. Using the classical model of what these price relationships should be, they could be imposed upon monopoly and big business by the government. The other goals, equality and freedom, would be established by other types of government regulation such as progressive income taxes and laws concerning the relationships between management, labor, stockholders, and the general public. But early thinking along classical lines about the control of business power did not go beyond the restoration by public regulation of the price and wage relationships that would "normally" prevail if there were free competition. It did not propose laws that would regulate the internal organization of business so as to restore some degree of individual economic freedom.

The attempt to restore the free competitive price system by government regulation can be called the *Public Utility Idea*. It stemmed from the early attempt of Progressives to regulate the railroads. Unduly high rates were being charged and discriminatory practices were being followed. The opposition of farmers led first to the establishment of state utility commissions, and finally to the Interstate Commerce Commission. The efforts of these commissions, however, to establish fair rates raised numerous questions as to what constituted fairness. In the end, the basic concept of fairness was a fair return, or profit, on a fairly-determined cost base. Although there were numerous differences as to the proper size of the cost base and the size of a fair return, the fundamental principle of a fair return remained as the theoretical guide for commissions, not only in the railroads, but also in other utility fields. *A fair return on minimum costs is what the classicists believed would result in any truly competitive market.* To regulate utilities in this way was to use *classical economics as the guide or goal of regulation.* Granted that railroads were really noncompetitive, that they were, in a sense, natural monopolies, the regulation consisted in restoring and maintaining the prices and output conditions which would presumably prevail if competition were feasible or existed. But what is a public utility? The closest approach to a definition is that public utilities are "industries affected with a public interest." But what is a public interest apart from the fact that the goods or services provided are of vital importance to the consumer? Many industries could be so described, and it is hard to draw the line. In the last analysis, drawing the line is probably based on how an industry behaves. If it violates basic economic goals, it is not acting in the public interest, and is thus "affected with a public interest." Prices should not be unduly high, costs should be low, and service and production should be efficient and ample in amount to meet public demand.

Whether or not the regulation of business and other solutions to the power problem should be in terms of classical economics, they should not follow goals which are purely pragmatic. Classicism purported to be a "scientific" description of the order and laws of the real world. In regulating business in terms of these laws, the rationalism of the eighteenth century implied that the purpose of government should be to maintain a natural order.

It may be that modern economics better describes the real economic world today than does classical theory, but we can still argue that regulation and power problem solutions should not be solely pragmatic. They should be guided by goals derived from an economics validly describing the world in which we live or want to live.

In summary, classical economics provides even today two valuable guides to the solution of our power problem. First, the goals of efficiency, freedom, equality, and balance are still the goals of economic freedom and democracy. They can become the basis of government regulation to curb power and restore at least the effects of freedom. Second, classical economics postulated that government action should be scientific in that it should not frustrate but obey "natural law." This amounts to saying that government action against concentrated power must have a scientific base, a new, valid socioeconomics. Classical economics does not provide this base although it establishes important goals for government regulation.

VII

The Economics of the New Deal

_____

THE long struggle against power which we traced in the preceding pages produced little that was new in social theory except the Public Utility Idea and some sporadic ideas of the New Deal brain trust. The struggle was largely political. The irresponsibility of big business was dramatized, the farmers were protected against monopolistic railroad rates, the trusts in general were curbed by antitrust legislation, the tariff was lowered to introduce more foreign competition, the monetary system was tinkered with to try to relieve debt burdens, and the New Deal provided relief and recovery through heavy government spending. First the Progressives and then the New Dealers abandoned belief in laissez-faire and stressed the concept of need. They both strongly favored economic regulation for the benefit of the common man. The New Deal strove to organize unorganized farmers and workers through government legislation so that they could gain greater economic power. But little was accomplished in reconstructing social theory.

The reconstruction is of prime importance. Despite promising beginnings during the administration of Wilson, and some of the ideas of the New Deal "brain trusters," we have not got ahead with the task. Liberals seem not to have learned that their function is more than merely to support the "angels." The essence of liberalism is intellectualism, and this has been true from the days of Jefferson. Unfortunately in the New Deal period, the "eggheads" came into disfavor, and Roosevelt himself disowned them. Liberalism lived and has continued to live on the intellectual capital created in the first two years of the Wilson and Roosevelt administrations, until this capital has become greatly dissipated. Intellectualism, as many politicians know, is politically dangerous. The liberals who followed in Roosevelt's footsteps from 1936 to the present have not been very courageous men.

Yet we can say that a new, courageous approach began with Wilson and grew again with the New Deal brain trust. Wilson supplied the basic ideas of restoring the *effects* and the *ideals* of individualism as reflected in economic competition. He also insisted that the solution of the average man's problems lay in an intellectual approach to these problems. Having explored the classical economics of Wilson, we need now to examine the intellectual originality, such as it was, of the New Deal. What was its contribution to the new socioeconomics which we so badly need?

First, it must be pointed out that the New Deal at least succeeded in changing the psychological tone of the nation. In 1933, economic conditions had reached a very low ebb, and fear and pessimism were widespread. Through Roosevelt's personality, expressed in his fireside chats, and the growing conviction that something would be or was being done, the fears and pessimism gradually subsided. The public was finally convinced that it had "nothing to fear but fear itself."

As fear dissolved, there were basic changes in the attitude of the public toward the government. For years, we had believed that the best government was the least government. These attitudes were derived partly from the traditions of the American Revolution, and partly from the teachings of

Adam Smith and David Ricardo. The economic system postulated by the classicists, as we have seen, was one of perfect efficiency and justice operating automatically through the laws of supply and demand. Any interference with it, said the classicists, could only make for inefficiency. Government was not in a position to improve on the laws of supply and demand and should keep its hands off business.

The New Deal made two major changes in these older attitudes. In the first place, it convinced the majority of the people that the laws of supply and demand could no longer work for our benefit without government intervention. In the second place, it convinced people also that government could act in the general interest, and that on the whole it could be relied upon to be benevolent. As John Kenneth Galbraith has put it, government came to be regarded by millions as a shield against adversity. It had now become the friend of the common man rather than the servant of the privileged few. Because of this new attitude toward government, the time was ripe for new political and economic theories as a basis for policy. Toward the end of the Roosevelt era, Professor Galbraith provided a new concept which synthesized much of the New Deal thinking along political and economic lines.

THE THEORY OF COUNTERVAILING POWER

Before 1929, there had been some signs of concern on the part of businessmen and liberals alike with respect to the fundamental soundness of our economic system. In each case, insecurity was dulled and almost relegated to the unconscious by the postwar prosperity from 1922 to 1929. Neither economists nor businessmen predicted the Great Depression. They ignored the seriousness of the underlying economic maladjustments of the twenties, and their faith in classicism made a severe depression inconceivable.

The insecurity of businessmen had to do with the inconsistency which existed between their beliefs about the economic system and its realities. According to the classical view, the best economic system was one of perfect competition, in which no seller had any great economic power. Without economic power, competition would protect the consumers and workers by insuring that prices were as low as possible, and production, wages, and employment as high as possible. There would be virtually no unemployment and the economic system would remain in balance with only slight ups and downs.

After the Civil War, however, competition had declined. In many fields, large-scale production and giant corporations appeared. Instead of individual businesses having no power, they came to have great power, and in setting prices and allocating resources they were not much disciplined by competition. Although profitable, these new conditions seemed wicked. They created a sense of guilt, since they violated the fundamental morality of economic classicism. The obvious reaction to this guilt was to deny them, to say that competition still prevailed, keeping prices as low as possible, and insuring maximum efficiency. From 1890 until 1917, it was hard to support these protestations because the whole sordid story of monopoly, privilege, and power had been brought out into the open by the Progressives. But with World War I and the postwar prosperity, the progressive movement died. It became possible for businessmen to insist without much dispute that a great amount of competition still existed. The success of this pretense was not enough, however, to remove the basic uneasiness of businessmen and others that an immoral, monopolistic economic system had crowded out a moral, competitive one.

In any power situation, the role of decision-making becomes important. When business was completely competitive, the free market made the decisions as to prices, output, the quantity and quality of goods, and all other economic matters. Theoretically, the businessman merely reacted to the decisions forced upon him by the market in much the way that the driver of an automobile reacts to red and green lights in traffic. Monopoly changed this, and economic decisions became the personal decisions of men who had attained positions of power. The question then arose in the minds of these men and the general public, by what right or authority were big businessmen to make the decisions? Did the authority come from God? Galbraith cites the statement of George F. Baer of the Reading Railroad, who said in part, in 1902, concerning his business activity, that "the rights and interests of the laboring man will be protected and cared for . . . by the Christian men to whom God in His infinite wisdom has given the control of the property interests of this country . . ." [1] Few businessmen were willing to concede, however, that they had great authority or that this authority was derived from God. They rather denied that they had great power or that they made their decisions personally without the compulsions of the "free" market. Nevertheless, there was an acute uneasiness among businessmen which became extreme when the catastrophe of 1929 was blamed on bad business decisions.

In view of this widespread belief, even on the part of businessmen, that they had made the decisions which caused the depression, one might have expected New Dealers to become "trustbusters." Businessmen derived the power to make wrong decisions because of trusts and the destruction of competition. If competition had prevailed, businessmen would have had to follow the changes in free-market prices determined by the all-wise laws of supply and demand. But except for the renewed and vigorous antitrust activity of Thurman Arnold after 1938, the New Deal made no serious attempt to restore competition and divest big business of its power to make important economic decisions. On the con-

[1] Galbraith, J. K., *American Capitalism*, pp. 61-62

trary, its efforts were in the opposite direction. As we have seen, the NRA, the AAA, and the Wagner Act were designed to create monopoly where it had not existed before.

The explanation of this *volte face* is to be found in the theory of countervailing power. Where great power has been created among buyers or sellers through oligopoly or oligopsony [1] this power may be offset by the development of monopoly among corresponding buyers or sellers. One example is the relationship between corporations and labor. To offset the power of the large manufacturers of steel as *buyers* of labor, the United Steel Workers Union might be regarded as a large monopoly of *sellers* of labor. Another example is the sale of groceries. The monopolistic position of *sellers* of food products has been offset by the establishment of great monopolistic *buyers* in the form of chain stores. Countervailing power provides protection against monopolistic power, not by restoring competition between the economic units on one side of the market, but by establishing competition of relative power equals *across* the market. The new monopoly situation may be among sellers, as in the example of labor given above, or it may be among buyers, as in the case of the chain stores. At any rate, a new kind of protective competition is established which acts across the market rather than on one side of it. The New Deal agricultural and labor programs may be said to have fostered group competition by creating countervailing power across the market. The NRA set up new situations of power and monopoly of small business to countervail the power of big business. This was countervailance, but on one side of the market.

The aspect of the New Deal which has proved mysterious is this turn toward monopoly. It seemed to contradict the trends of the liberal or progressive movement which had

[1] Oligopoly: control of the market by a few sellers; oligopsony: control of the market by a few buyers.

been anti-monopolistic. The New Deal position becomes less inconsistent with progressivism when thought of as an attempt to provide protection for the weak by creating a new form of competition. At this point, the Galbraith terms of *original* and *secondary* monopoly come into play. Where a monopoly or oligopoly already exists ("original" monopoly) the progressive has a choice of breaking up the monopoly or of setting up a rival and competing monopoly across the market ("secondary" monopoly). For the most part, the Roosevelt Administration took monopoly or oligopoly for granted. Except for the vigorous efforts of Thurman Arnold, the New Deal days were not noted for trust-busting. The main policy of protection was the creation of secondary monopoly to offset original monopoly.

Presumably secondary monopoly should not be prohibited under the antitrust laws because it is a *remedy* for monopoly. For example, the Norris-LaGuardia Act excluded labor activities from attack under the antitrust laws, and New Deal Supreme Courts extended this exclusion. The AAA of 1933 accomplished the same result for farmer organizations. Inconsistency developed, however, when some farmer cooperatives such as the California Fruit Growers Exchange were charged with monopoly. Similarly, the food chains which were providing countervailing power on behalf of the consumer against the large sellers of food products were attacked under the antitrust laws. Consistency would require that the antitrust laws apply only to original monopoly.

The development of countervailing power with the assistance of the government under Roosevelt can be defended as having improved the economic status and welfare of both farmers and organized workers, the principal backers of the New Deal. It can be argued also that the development of countervailing monopolistic power was a means of removing two less-recognized evils of monopoly: (1) the depression, and (2) the politically unchecked power situation resulting from original monopoly. The ability of monopolies to raise prices of industrial products without a corresponding rise in wages and farm prices threw the economy badly out of balance and was a main contributor to the depression of 1929. The unchecked power of big business before farmers and workers were organized to offset it was politically unhealthy. Any power situation is bad when it results in both economic and political unbalance.

Although countervailing power should have reduced the feeling of insecurity about the economic system experienced by both businessmen and liberals, the insecurity persisted. As Galbraith points out, businessmen did not relish the notion that their great use of power was made innocuous because it was now countered by the power of unions. They did not approve of union power, and they were dubious also about the desirability of organized farm pressures. They preferred, even after World War II, to insist that the economic system was still competitive. Belief in its competitive nature became an article of faith and they bemoaned the loss of this faith so much that the National Manufacturers Association undertook a campaign to restore belief in the principles of free enterprise. Liberals, on their part, could not themselves regard countervailing power as freeing the economic system from all need for regulation in the interests of the general public. Either more vigorous efforts had to be made to break monopoly in those areas where countervailing power could not be developed, or outright regulation along the old lines of the progressive movement should be extended.

THE LIMITS OF COUNTERVAILING POWER

Galbraith, the originator of the concept of countervailing power, is not certain that it solves the power problem in the economic world. He has merely contended that at many points the power of monopoly has been offset, and that a new form of competition partly counters the power of original monopoly. The offsetting power is not the complete answer to undue monopoly power. He notes three situations in which countervailing power may prove ineffective: (1) where it cannot be organized to offset original power; (2) where it is expected to result, like free competition, in decisions which would lead to the greatest balance and efficiency in the economy; and (3) where there is inflation and an unlimited demand for products.

The primary difficulty in assuming that countervailing power can be the answer to the American power problem lies really in the first of these situations. Probably only a quarter to a third of the labor force is readily organizable. If this is true, the vast majority of the labor force is left unprotected against the great power of business monopoly. Labor leaders sometimes assume that organized labor protects unorganized labor. But does it? The effect of labor organization may be to raise the wages of the organized part of the labor force without in any way raising unorganized workers' wages at the same time. The wages of the unorganized may even fall as a result of the need to raise the wages of organized labor.

The farmers also are a minority group. Countervailing power increases and maintains the prices of farm products. The resulting rise in food costs may not be of great concern to organized labor since it is able to raise its incomes. But what of the fate of the large majority of labor which is unorganized? Are they not paying for the welfare of both the farmer and the organized worker? Perhaps it can be argued that the unorganized worker is a consumer, and that food chains and other large retail organizations afford them protection as consumers from the farmers and the food processors. The food chains may have reduced prices below what they would have been if all retailers had been independents and had operated as numerous individual buyers of food in competition with the powerful food processors, but the original optimism of Galbraith and others about counter-vailing power was probably too great. The food chains them-selves are monopolistic *vis-à-vis* the individual consumer. They are an oligopoly of sellers, as far as the housewife who patronizes them is concerned.

It must also be emphasized that countervailing power is merely a *check* on the power of monopoly and oligopoly. It is not a *substitute* for the classical model of a competitive free enterprise economy. The classical model was an ideal economic system providing maximum efficiency through ideal resource allocation because prices were set at the lowest possible average total cost plus a minimum profit and at the point of maximum production and employment. There is no guarantee that in the competition between a monopoly of sellers and a monopoly of buyers, prices and output will be set at the points of lowest costs and maximum output. The conclusions of Chamberlain and Robinson, who worked out systems of price theory under assumptions of monopolistic competition and oligopoly are that prices will be higher under monopolistic competition than under free competition, and that resource allocation will be considerably less than perfect. Where oligopolies of buyers compete with oligopo-lies of sellers, there is no certainty that the results will equal those of free competition. It is likely only that prices will be lower and output higher than would be the case if there was only an oligopoly of sellers.

Finally, as to the effectiveness of countervailing power in a period of inflation, Galbraith has grave misgivings. After World War II, we had inflation until 1956. The economy grew up to the inflation unleashed in 1946 and during the Korean War, and the rate of capital investment for a while declined. It may be that the nineteen sixties will not be very inflationary. But it is certain that countervailing power proves of little value during inflation. The reason is best illustrated by considering what happens when a strong union like the United Steel Workers bargains with a strong corporation like the United States Steel Corporation during a period of inflation. Since it is relatively easy for the steel company to pass on higher wage payments in the form of higher steel prices, the bargaining for higher wages may actually force up the price of steel. The consumer has no protection. Organized labor and organized business get together to benefit themselves against the interests of the rest of the economy, *which is the majority of the economy*. There is, moreover, no check upon the exercise of power against the general interest. The President of the United States can counsel restraint, as Eisenhower did during the fifth round in the price-wage spiral in steel in 1952, but no one has power to *compel* restraint.

KEYNESIANISM

The Roosevelt administration may have promoted the well-being of special groups like farmers and organized labor to some extent through the development of countervailing power. But the *average man* was benefitted, and economic recovery was brought about, almost entirely through the practice of deficit spending. Capitalism was "saved" through deficit spending. The theory behind deficit spending is found in the economics of John Maynard Keynes, and the unconscious adoption of some aspects of Keynesian economics is the only significant contribution of New Dealers to the solution of the power problem.[1]

It has been said that probably the greatest achievement of Keynes was the demolition of Say's Law. The basic premise of Keynes was that supply does *not* create its own demand. Put another way, there is no built-in mechanism in

[1] Long after deficit spending became an established policy forced upon the New Deal by unbalanced budgets, New Dealers began to rationalize that they had consciously followed Keynesian economic theory. Conservatives accepted this belief and attacked the New Deal by attacking Keynesianism.

the economic system by which purchasing power is sustained. Thus there can be shortage of money purchasing power leading to unemployment of both men and capital. It follows from this that there need not be an equilibrium in the economy at full employment. The economy may balance below full employment, or there may be inflation, a balance above the level of money demand needed for full employment. Keynes believed that instead of full employment being the norm, either depression levels or inflation might be just as common in an economy, and therefore just as normal.

The starting point in the increase or creation of national income, Keynes argued, was an increase in money demand. By purchasing goods with money, or spending, employment and production were called into existence. Demand thus created supply; supply did not create demand, as posited in the classical sequence. Hence the paramount importance of spending. The New Dealers discovered that only through increasing money spending through national government deficits could they lift the economy out of the depression. It is doubtful that they did this because they believed in the Keynesian doctrine, but once having done it, they defended their actions by citing the doctrine.

Keynes divided spending into four major parts: consumer spending, investment spending, foreign spending, and government spending. Let us give these four forms of spending the letters C, I, F, and G, in the same order. Then C plus I plus F plus G equals the gross national product or total national expenditure (NE). Of these forms of spending, Keynes had a predilection for I, or investment. The normal or traditional way for recovery or economic growth to come about under capitalism was through the growth of investment. To stimulate investment, government might play an active role by lowering interest rates or business taxes and by creating a favorable psychological climate for investment. If recovery or high level production came about through the growth of investment, the economy would be following the normal patterns of the capitalist system. But in addition, early Keynesianism assumed that investment spending, in contrast to other forms of spending, led to a multiplication of production and income.

Keynes, like the classicists, believed in equilibrium in the economic system. He differed from them in that he did not believe in an equilibrium set automatically at the level of full employment. It could be reached above or below this level. The process of reaching a level had to do with rates of saving and the amount of investment. An illustration may make the meaning of Keynesian equilibrium clearer.

Let us assume that the amount of spending needed to reach full employment in the economy is $500 billion. This figure may be the result of many calculations and assumptions. We may assume a labor force of 72,000,000 people employed at various wage levels and the expenditure of money on interest, rents, and profits at certain amounts. Granted these assumptions, the economy must spend $500 billion or there will be unemployment. Let us assume that the actual expenditures of the economy are only $400 billion, resulting in much unemployment. In order to reach full employment, there must be more expenditure. How much expenditure will be required? Will $10 billion of new investment be enough? Hardly, since $10 billion of additional investment, even if it multiplies in effect enough to create $30 billion of new consumer income, will raise national income only to $430 billion. There will still be many unemployed workers. If investment income multiplies consumer income three times, however, an investment of $33.3 billion would raise total income to $500 billion, and full employment would be achieved at this point of equilibrium. But an investment larger than this amount would cause inflation.

To summarize, equilibrium in the economy is not necessarily reached at full employment. It may occur below, causing unemployment, or it may occur above, causing inflation. An increase in national income arises mainly from additional investment spending. The amount of income increase arising from this spending will depend on the amount of multiplication of income resulting from the spending.

The New Deal followed Keynesianism in that, through deficits, it greatly increased spending. To be sure, these expenditures were not investments, but they multiplied in rounds of spending in much the same way as investment spending, the national income increased, and unemployment fell from 14,000,000 in 1933 to 8,000,000 in 1939. Although this decrease in unemployment was remarkable, New Deal spending was insufficient to create full employment. Not until World War II was spending great enough to reach this goal. But by 1942 we had reached it. Unfortunately, we went beyond it, and prepared the way for the great inflation of 1946. The huge deficits in the war years 1943, 1944, and 1945, caused a tremendous postwar rise in prices once price controls were removed.

Through Keynesian methods, the Roosevelt Administration was able to (1) bring the country out of the depths of the depression, (2) create full employment, and (3) finance our greatest war. But most important, it was able to demonstrate that depressions are unnecessary if government is willing to adopt appropriate fiscal and monetary policies and to act promptly. The Roosevelt Administration's attempt to make Keynesian theory a permanent basis for economic policy fostered the Employment Act passed in 1946.

THE EMPLOYMENT ACT OF 1946

During and immediately after World War II, men in all walks of life—economists, politicians, union leaders, and business executives—feared a postwar depression. To ward it off, Keynesian doctrine was virtually enacted into law. The preamble of the Employment Act states that "it is the continuing policy and responsibility of the Federal Government to use all practicable means consistent with (free enterprise) . . . and other essential considerations of national policy . . . to promote maximum employment, production, and purchasing power." Thus the government went on record against laissez-faire and the theory of automatic adjustment through the price system. It assumed responsibility for fighting depressions. To do this, a Council of Economic Advisers was established, under the President, to advise as to the means of implementing the Act, to collect data, and to formulate a national economic budget. This council, consisting of three economists, is appointed by the President, and prepares his economic budget, which must be submitted to Congress each year along with the regular budget. The economic budget is essentially a measure of the trends in spending, in line with Keynesian theory. From various sources, such as data on the gross national product, gross private domestic investment, and expenditure by all levels of government, a national budget is compiled, showing expenditures for the whole economy on one side, classified as consumer, business, and government expenditures, and showing income from these sources on the other side. Trends in expenditures balanced against the income figures are used as a means of predicting future changes in expenditure and the need for various kinds of action to maintain full employment or to prevent inflation. The budget is the basis of presidential recommendations to Congress in carrying out the purposes of the act.

Various difficulties have been experienced in administering the act. For one thnig, the past record of several years of national expenditure is not a sure guide in predicting future expenditures. Trends may change. In addition, the percentage relations between the different components of the budget change. If they remained fixed, predictions could be more readily made. In addition, there has been considerable political opposition to the functioning of the Council. In spite of the recognition of federal responsibility for maintaining employment, not all recommendations to achieve this goal are palatable. For example, a provision in one of the original drafts of the law allowed the President to *recommend* an unbalanced budget. This provision was deleted. Finally, it is easy enough to get Congress to accept proposals to cope with a depression because they mainly involve more spending. Proposals requiring higher taxation to check inflation are very unpopular. Roosevelt had an easy enough time obtaining support for his policies, but Truman's high tax program to curb inflation encountered much opposition.

SUMMARY

In summary, the New Deal began pragmatically to cope with the problems of the Great Depression and World War II. In these essentially experimental efforts, it evolved two types of policy: the application of countervailing power, and deficit spending. Although the New Deal succeeded in restoring a degree of prosperity and in achieving a level of full employment during the war, it made the problem of power in the United States worse by organizing new power groups and encouraging competition for power on a larger organized scale. Neither countervailing power nor Keynesianism taken by themselves have provided an answer for the American power problem. In short, the New Deal made capitalism work by restoring prosperity and provided billions of dollars of much-needed relief to farmers and the unemployed, but it by no means restored individualism and freedom to the American people. Truman, Eisenhower, and Kennedy were to inherit from Roosevelt a power problem which intensified and became acute largely because of postwar inflation. Although, as we shall point out more fully, both Keynesian economics and the theory of countervailing power contribute concepts germane to the new socioeconomics which is needed, they are not, taken by themselves, the answer to our great problem of power. This is due partly to our present problem of inflation since inflation creates a new matrix in which the power struggle operates. But it is due also to the development of an economy of affluence. Thus, before we can go farther in our search for a new socioeconomic theory which will be adequate to cope with the power problem, we must digress to trace the recent history of inflation and the growth of affluence as factors in the power struggle.

VIII

Inflation and the Power Problem:
Truman and Eisenhower

I N THE years following World War II, the American economy experienced a transition from scarcity to affluence and full employment. In spite of deficit spending, unemployment had not been reduced below 8,000,000 before 1939. But the war brought unemployment down to 700,000. The gross national product rose from $91 billion in 1939 to $213 billion in 1945. Thus the problems of the postwar period became those of a full employment economy tending toward inflation with only minor recessions and a high and rapidly rising standard of living. They were also the problems of an economy in which defense production played a major role. A new power struggle and new political alignments centered around inflation, the problem of affluence, the rate of economic growth, and expenditures for national defense. The old political alliance which accounted for Roosevelt's tremendous following broke down. The Keynesian approach and the theory of countervailing power proved inadequate to cope with postwar problems, especially inflation. An analysis of the postwar inflation problem and how it was handled will enable us to advance further in our attempt to develop a new socioeconomic theory.

INFLATION OR DEPRESSION?

Due to the enormous spending by the Federal Government on the war, reaching an annual total of $100.5 billion in 1945, a large backlog of purchasing power was accumulated in the form of bank savings and government bonds. Immediately after the war, these savings threatened to disgorge into the regular channels of spending. Millions had denied themselves various kinds of consumer goods such as automobiles and refrigerators. There was a great urge to catch up on unsatisfied consumer desires. But in spite of this situation, some economists predicted depression instead of inflation. A great cutback in federal military expenditures was thought to be inevitable. Economists feared a reduction of $50 billion or more in federal spending, with a rise in private spending of not more than $20 or $30 billion. Moreover, past precedent decreed that the war be followed by a major depression, as in 1920-1921.

The true nature of the postwar economic situation, however, was not long in doubt. Although a recession occurred in 1946, it was mild, and unemployment rose to only 5,000,000. The recession could be attributed to the frictions involved in business reconversion, the shift from military to civilian employment, and a drop in federal expenditures. Instead of a great reduction in the federal budget, however, federal expenditures remained in 1946 at the high figure of $65.1 billion. By 1947, a boom had set in, and a sharp inflation which began in 1946 was to continue until 1948.

THE DECLINE OF THE GRAND ALLIANCE

President Truman was to have his difficulties in attempting to control inflation on behalf of the general public. Presumably he had inherited from Franklin Roosevelt a political alignment which had proved unbeatable in the elections of 1932, 1936, 1940, and 1944. This "Grand Alliance" consisted of most of the farmers, organized labor, miscellaneous sections of the lower middle class, the poor, a large part of the aged, the liberal intellectuals, and many small businessmen. But in the Roosevelt years after 1935 the nation became increasingly conservative, and some supporters of his administration deserted. The weakening of his following began in 1934 and 1935 when many people reacted against the relief system as excessive spending for the unemployed without work or contribution in return. Others severly criticized the Agricultural Adjustment Act. Still others were incensed by the regulations of the NRA and the supposed undue influence of "pinks," "reds," and "eggheads" on the White House.

Good politician that he was, Roosevelt was not averse to throwing overboard some of his left-wing support, and he began to appease his critics by shifting legislative and administrative policy to the political right. The substitution of the WPA, which required those on relief to work for their money; the adoption of the Social Security Act, which introduced unemployment insurance based on past earnings; and the attempt to balance the budget through receipts from payroll taxes, in 1937, were all measures moving the New Deal to a more conservative position. The effect was the dulling of criticism, and the achievement of an even more overwhelming public support for the administration in 1936 than it had received in 1932.

But as the country got out of the depression into years of relative prosperity, criticism and disaffection grew even more, despite the skillful efforts of Roosevelt to hold his enormous following. The agricultural program, the mounting public debt, the continuation of deficits, his partiality toward organized labor, and his attempt to pack a recalcitrant Supreme Court whittled away the Grand Alliance, and Roosevelt had to campaign hard in 1940 against the liberal Republican Wendell Willkie. The war created further problems for the alliance, and caused disaffection even among liberals.

Fundamental in explaining Truman's difficulties in coping with inflation and other postwar problems were the breakdown of the Roosevelt Grand Alliance and the inadequacies of New Deal economics. An almost equal division of the voters between the Democratic and Republican parties had developed. The equality of this division was somewhat obscured by the large vote received by General Eisenhower in his two elections, but it was evident in Congress and in the tight election of President Kennedy in 1960. What changes caused the breakdown of the Grand Alliance? They may be summarized as follows: (1) The decline in the political power of organized labor, which could no longer obtain the support of a large segment of unorganized labor. (2) The split between large and small farmers, who differed in their views as to the Government's farm program. (3) The split of voters generally over inflation—some benefiting from it and therefore opposing price controls, others being harmed by it and favoring measures to prevent it. (4) The rising concern over civil rights and racial discrimination, which alienated large sections of southern voters who had supported Roosevelt. (Fortunately for him, Roosevelt was able to avoid this issue.) (5) The growing concern over communism and the fear that the Democrats were too soft on communists. (6) The growing antagonism of the unorganized public against the power and tactics of organized labor, which was identified in their minds with the Democratic party. (7) The fear that Keynesianism had been carried too far and the belief that a new "normalcy" was needed in which business men would control the economic policies of the Federal Government. (8) The growing conservatism that always results from sustained prosperity. (9) The tremendously successful public relations campaigns of the large corporations, and the belief of millions of voters that the Federal Government should be favorable to big business.

As a result of these changes, a man who was basically a political liberal like Truman could not move vigorously in liberal directions, at least not consistently. Similarly, the Republican party could not be wholly or consistently conservative. The forces had become too equally divided. For this reason Senator Taft, although aptly described as "Mr. Republican," could not even obtain the nomination of the Republican party. In addition, the Republican party, although theoretically opposed to the New Deal social legislation and to Keynesianism, had to accept and even extend both when it captured the Presidency under Eisenhower.

THE PRICE-WAGE FABRIC

Neither Truman nor Eisenhower, when faced with severe inflation in an affluent economy, was able to rely on the economic theories of the New Deal. Inflation as an economic phenomenon gives rise to many different opinions and points of view. The older classical view of inflation found its cause merely in the overextension of the money supply and its evil in the unfair redistribution of income and wealth resulting from rising prices. This theory of inflation presumed a free competitive price system in which any rise in the volume of money could only result in a rise in prices. The newer, or Keynesian, view of inflation was to attribute it only to a rising money supply *in periods of full or near-full employment.* But in the Truman and Eisenhower administrations a new evil of inflation had developed which was not understood and which could not be met by applying either Keynesian or classical economics. The trouble with the Keynesian analysis of the causes of both depression and inflation was its assumption of the current price and wage structure as a static background in which saving-investment dynamics operate. To be more specific, if it can be assumed that at a given time the amount of spending in the economy requisite to the achievement of full employment is $500 billion, we can readily understand why investment at certain amounts and certain accompanying rates of saving will result in, say, $400 billion of spending and 10,000,000 unemployed, or $450 billion of spending and 5,000,000 unemployed, or even $600 billion of spending, little unemployment, and serious inflation. But this arbitrarily assumes that *full employment requires $500 billion of spending and that the $500 billion figure is a fixed amount, the causes of which can be ignored.* But what creates the $500 billion figure?

Obviously the answer lies in the price and wage fabric which has been established at any given time. It is a huge complex of individual, business, corporate, union, and governmental decisions and agreements, arrived at either through buying and selling in the market place or through administrative decisions in the offices of unions, businesses, or governments. It can even result in part from customs as to prices and wages, from legislative fixations, from the rulings of public utility commissions, or from *sub rosa* price-fixing agreements. No one can conceive of this vast complex of income and price interrelations as permanently frozen. It may not be as dynamic as investment and rates of saving, but it changes. In some ways, the changes in this price-wage fabric have more to do with the causes of inflation or depression than the flow of the volume of money income through the channels of investment, saving, and consumption about which Keynes was primarily concerned.

Our assertion is especially pertinent in connection with inflation. The postwar period gives much evidence of this. Once the lid of control was removed in 1946 by the repeal of OPA, the money purchasing power, which enormously exceeded the volume of civilian production after the war, caused one of the sharpest inflations in history. The 1939 consumer price index of the U.S. Department of Labor rose from 140 in 1945 to 152 by the end of 1946, to 185 by the end of 1947, and to over 200 by the end of 1948. In three years prices had gone up more than forty percent or by an average of about fourteen percent a year. One can look at the situation as a huge avalanche of buying power which pushed the full employment price-wage fabric from a $200 billion to a $300 or $400 billion level in a very short time. From a human and institutional standpoint it caused a mad scramble in price-wage relations to bring about an increase in various component incomes as rapid as the rise in prices. Looked at from yet another standpoint, it created a great struggle for power which expressed itself as a struggle for purchasing power.

The struggle most publicized was that between large corporations and large unions. The plethora of money buying power had its first effect in raising prices in competitive markets and in decisions of large corporations to raise their administered prices. The second effect was to cause labor and salaried employees to demand higher wages and incomes. Since unemployment was not very great in 1946, most employees were in a relatively strong bargaining position, and could threaten to quit or strike. They were able to exercise the power which comes from withholding a desired economic service. But particularly potent in this respect was organized labor. Weak were government employees and other groups with relatively fixed incomes. Completely impotent were those living on pensions or investments, except insofar as they were able to exert influence on government to raise pensions or could sell fixed investments and transfer their money into stocks or mutual funds.

THE WARTIME STRUGGLE OVER WAGES AND PRICES

In the struggle over higher wages, the stage was set during the war. When the war began, there were 9,000,000 unemployed, and even in 1942 the number was as high as 4,000,000. It was thought that unemployment of this large amount would prevent inflationary pressures for higher wages. But by January 1942 average hourly wages had risen twenty-two percent above the level of 1939. It became apparent that if the Federal Government were to curb the wage factor in inflation it would have to adopt a fixed policy as to wage increases. The administration could not, however, bring itself to establish direct wage controls immediately. This was too unpopular. But something had to be done. The immediate action was the establishment in 1942 of the National War Labor Board. This body consisted of four representatives each, from management, labor, and the general public. It was not set up to fix wage ceilings. Its functions were primarily (1) to settle labor disputes in order to keep at a minimum strikes and work stoppages that would hamper the war effort, and (2) to arbitrate or settle disputes which could not be settled without recourse to the board. In 1942, labor disputes multiplied, and the board was caught between the pressure of unions demanding wage increases to offset the rising cost of living, and the strictures of the OPA against raising wages where the rise would push against price ceilings.

Because the War Labor Board was not able to cope with the many disputes that were arising, it appealed to President Roosevelt for the determination of a new wage policy. The task was delegated to the Bureau of the Budget, which proposed that wages be frozen as of April 1942. The War Labor Board, however, was unable to go this far, and as an alternative established the "Little Steel Formula" in July of that year. Wage increases were to be allowed (1) to remove inequalities, (2) to raise wages that were substandard, and (3) to raise wages fifteen percent above the level of January 1, 1941. The Little Steel Formula governed wage policy until the end of the war.[1] In October 1942 the board had its hands strengthened by a ruling of the Office of Economic Stabilization that no further wage increases could be allowed except for pur-

[1] Chandler, Lester V., *Inflation in the United States, 1940-1948*, p. 333

poses of correcting inequalities or substandard conditions. Despite these apparently rigid restrictions on wages, so many cases for increases could be covered under the correction of "inequities" that wages rose sixteen percent between October 1942 and July 1945. Total wage increases between January 1941 and July 1945 amounted to forty percent.[1]

The flexibility of wage policy indicated by the forty percent wage rise was not sufficient to satisfy organized labor. As Chandler points out, labor wanted an increase in wages which would exactly equal the rising cost of living. In other words, it wanted the War Labor Board to adopt an "escalator clause." In addition, it wanted an upward revision in the cost of living index which it claimed underestimated the degree of the inflation. No account was taken in the index of the disappearance of low cost goods and the deterioration in the quality of goods. Also, labor was not willing to accept the higher actual incomes due to overtime and steadier employment as a sufficient compensation for higher living costs. In terms of actual purchasing power from higher incomes, organized labor was better off in 1943 than it had been before the war. But it wanted more income regardless of the adverse effects upon other parts of the employed population. Its objective was *higher hourly rates* which would rise as much as a cost of living index, revised considerably upward. The political power of organized labor, exerted without too much regard for the general interest, was almost great enough to achieve this goal. Only through the delaying tactics of the War Labor Board and the tightening of price controls by the OPA was the drive for still higher wages halted.

In insisting on inflationary price rises in their own interest and to the detriment of the general interest, organized farmers were even more avaricious than organized labor. Farm groups fought bitterly all attempts to curb the rise in

[1] *Ibid.,* p. 335

food prices. They insisted that the inflationary situation of the war should be taken advantage of to bring farm prices into line with industrial prices. It was pointed out that in 1941 farm prices were depressed relative to industrial prices. But organized labor and farmers ignored the fact that the wages of perhaps thirty million other workers had lagged behind the price rises which they had helped to promote. Fortunately, some semblance of the general interest was preserved by the War Labor Board and the OPA. According to Chandler, "If wage rates had been permitted to escalate with food prices, and farm prices to escalate with the prices of industrial products (in whose costs labor was the most important single factor) the inflationary spiral could have been greatly encouraged." [1]

With the end of the war, wage controls were relaxed and finally removed altogether. The pressure of organized labor for the removal of wage controls became extreme and paralleled the great demand for the removal of all controls expressed by other parts of the population. The Truman administration made efforts to stem the tide for decontrol, but failed. Labor argued that reconversion would cause a great decline in labor income from the loss of jobs, the loss of overtime pay, and the downgrading of many war workers into lower paid civilian jobs. Higher wages were needed not only to compensate for these changes but to prevent a depression due to the collapse of purchasing power. This was the position taken by George Meany of the American Federation of Labor.

Through a series of executive orders, wage rises were permitted to compensate for the rise in the cost of living from 1941 to 1945. Increases of eighteen and a half percent were regarded as standard. Wage rises could then be used by employers to obtain compensatory price increases from the OPA. After the situation had become chaotic and the lines

[1] *Ibid.,* pp. 337-338

against neither wage nor price increases were being held, an executive order in November 1946 removed all wage controls and most price controls. It remained only for Congress to abolish formally the War Labor Board and OPA.

A power struggle between organized labor and corporations then began which resulted in wage and compensatory price increases. Ultimately, it resulted also in an unholy alliance between labor and management to cooperate in causing both wage and price rises. But the wage-price struggle went through three rounds under Truman before the lesson of cooperation was learned.

The first round in the battle occurred in 1946. Labor was represented by the great CIO unions, notably in steel and automobiles. The unions demanded fifty-two hours' pay for a forty hour week, a thirty percent increase in wage rates. The corporations countered with arguments that labor productivity had not increased by thirty percent, and that wages could not be increased beyond the increase in labor productivity without forcing the corporations to raise prices. The disputes were settled by agreement on the standard eighteen-and-a-half-percent increase in wages permitted by the War Labor Board during the war. Industrial prices were raised in compensation.

Price increases resulting from labor disputes and the further increases resulting from the demise of OPA left labor in a worse position in 1947 than in 1946. The cost of living rose to levels that more than offset the eighteen-and-a-half-percent rise in hourly wage rates. As a result, a second round in the battle began in 1947. The large CIO unions, which again led the fight, once more demanded a thirty percent increase in wages, but subsequently reduced their demands to an increase of 15 cents an hour. As a result, the price-wage spiral began a second time. By the end of 1947, however, labor was again back where it started. Wage rises did not fully compensate for price rises. This led to the third round of the battle in 1948, in which labor was able to obtain wage increases of 11 to 13 cents an hour.[1]

A number of conclusions can be drawn from the history that we have described. (1) It is apparent that organized labor was able during the war to obtain a forty percent compensation for rising living costs. (2) After the war, organized labor managed to keep up with the rising cost of living by three wage-price rounds, and by 1948 was even a little ahead. (3) Even before the abolition of OPA, large corporations were able to offset wage rises by price rises. (4) The pressure of organized labor for higher wages, of corporations for even higher increases in prices, and of farmers for price supports and high OPA ceilings succeeded in causing a wage-price spiral of very serious proportions. (5) The majority of the population, consisting of unorganized labor, small business, and persons living on fixed incomes—the small, average or common men—were brutally sacrificed to the interests of organized labor, big farmers, and large corporations. (6) A great unfair redistribution of income thus resulted, hurting millions of powerless ordinary individuals. Only gradually, and by no means completely, were the resulting inequities rectified after 1948. (7) The economic losses of unorganized labor and small business turned voters away from the Democratic party and caused them to question the liberalism of New Dealers who stood by organized labor in its efforts to secure an income advantage over the unorganized parts of the population. These disaffected voters were only too anxious to support management's attack on labor tactics, and the partiality of the National Labor Relations Board. One result was the enactment of the Taft-Hartley Act. When these factors in political change are properly as-

[1] *Ibid.*, pp. 338-344

sessed, it is not hard to understand why Eisenhower swept the country in 1952. His personality was not the only explanation of the Republican victory. The *Grand Alliance had been seriously deteriorated by the wage-price struggle during and immediately after World War II.*

THE PRICE-WAGE FABRIC AND DEPRESSION

In terms of economic theory, the history of the wage-price power struggle was a rise in the full employment price-wage fabric in response to the inflationary effect of the postwar plethora of purchasing power. The institutional forces of organized farmers, organized workers, and large corporations proceeded to rewrite the fabric upward to at least $400 billion. The unorganized parts of the fabric were gradually upwritten also in response to the inflation achieved in the organized sectors of the economy.

The upwriting of the price-wage fabric when there is excess money income is an inevitable economic process. It does not usually proceed uniformly, however, and the rise in the overall total of the fabric may go too far. The lack of uniformity in the upwriting leads to the kinds of injustice for which inflation has been criticized. These evils taken by themselves are serious enough. But the lack of uniformity in the upwriting, and the possibility of overwriting, are productive of unbalance and an actual shortage of the purchasing power needed for full employment and for sustained economic growth. As Galbraith was impelled to conclude, countervailing power is an ineffective remedy for these ills. As a matter of fact, there has been no countervailing power at all since the late forties, because organized labor and big business learned to join hands in their mutual efforts, one to raise wages, the other, prices.

As we have pointed out earlier, organized labor got ahead of the cost of living in the third price round. In fact, the decline in Federal expenditures and the actual overwriting of the price-wage fabric by 1948 brought inflation to a sharp halt. Prices fell in 1949. More serious, however, was the development of a severe recession. The recession of 1949 marked a temporary halt in the great postwar boom. At this juncture, the American economy threatened to decline.

Two factors restored the upward rise in 1951. The first of these was the adoption of the Marshall Plan, which increased Federal spending by providing $12 billion of aid to Europe. Foreign aid acts as an increase in investment and an export stimulus. It is one of the Keynesian devices to restore full employment. The other and more effective means of restoring recovery, boom, and growth was the outbreak of the Korean War. But the war brought with it the resumption of serious inflation because Truman was unwilling or unable to use price controls immediately. The consumer price index rose in 1951 from 198 to 213. In 1952 it rose further to 218. Behind the inflation was the marked rise in Federal spending. By 1952, annual Federal expenditures had risen to $67 billion.

The resumption of greater spending and the rise in inflation resulted in a further upwriting of the price-wage fabric. In the price rounds that followed the inflationary surge, there was overwriting. This fact, together with the ending of the Korean War by Eisenhower, led to the recession of 1953, the longest and strangest decline to occur in the postwar period. The bottom was not reached until 1955.

The recession of 1953 is notable in that it could not be explained by a shortage of purchasing power. Never before in the history of the nation had a depression or recession been accompanied by ample money purchasing power and by an actual continuation of price rises several months after the recession began. To many it seemed the oddest of all recessions. *It marked the beginning of a new era in which a potentially full employment economy could go into recession because of one aspect of the inflation process, the overwrit-*

ing of the price-wage fabric. It can be called the first INFLA-TION DEPRESSION. No shortage of money incomes could possibly explain it. Federal expenditures had risen in 1953 to the all-time peacetime peak of $77 billion. But even with the highest peacetime gross national product ever reached in the United States, a recession occurred. Put in another way, the explanation is that *business and labor had priced themselves out of the market.* Even the enormous purchasing power could not equal the total of the price-wage fabric needed for full employment.

The point can be illustrated by the use of data for the period. In 1953 the gross national product was $360.5 billion. The probable amount of spending then needed for full employment due to the overwriting of the price-wage fabric was $380 to $400 billion. Power pressure groups had so boosted prices and wages that even with the greatest spending in the nation's history neither full employment nor growth could be sustained. *And in this lies the great modern danger in the concentration of economic power in the hands of unions and large corporations, a danger which threatens either to stagnate the economy and choke off growth, or to cause periodic depressions.*

EISENHOWER AND INFLATION

In 1953, when Eisenhower succeeded Truman as President, new anti-inflation policies were followed. Although the Democrats could not continue price control after World War II, and had used it reluctantly and to a limited extent during the Korean War, they had at least reduced the size of the federal budget and had maintained high taxes. These budgetary policies, which were aimed at a reduction or at least a stabilization of consumer income and demand, are known as *fiscal policies.* The Republicans, sensing the unpopularity of fiscal policy, opposed it in the election of 1952. They contended that fiscal policy is both harmful and unnecessary as an inflation control device. In its place, they promised to return (1) to *monetary policies* and (2) to "leadership" and "moral suasion." These promises undoubtedly added to the votes received by General Eisenhower in 1952.

Monetary policy (called by Galbraith the "monetary illusion") had been highly respected before World War I and its prestige lingered into the twenties. Basically, it meant the control of the flow of income by actions taken by the central bank. The Bank of England's control over the discount rate was the world's leading example of the use of monetary policy. By raising the bank discount rates, borrowing could be discouraged and the supply of credit reduced. Assuming that inflation is caused by too much money income, the reduction of money income that takes the form of bank money was regarded as a highly effective control. Faith in the Bank's monetary power was unreasoned and resembled belief in miracles. The degree of faith was in direct proportion to ignorance concerning these "mysteriously effective" bank powers. The Great Depression, however, brought disillusionment. The Bank was no longer regarded as omnipotent, and monetary policy was rudely "debunked." Raising interest rates has little effect on investment or consumer spending when the prospects of high profits and prosperity remain good. Monetary policy as a device for the control of overall national expenditures had been discarded by the time of World War II. Monetary policy, however, has the great advantage of political feasibility. It avoids the use of such painful fiscal measures as raising taxes, or price and wage controls.

Except through the decision to end the Korean War, the Eisenhower administration had little success in checking inflation. A major reason for ill success was the entry of big business representatives into high places in the government and the general atmosphere of cooperation with business, especially big business. Businessmen wanted to settle labor disputes by raising both prices and wages. The government, which had become business-minded owing to the infiltration of business into the administration, wanted to accept the wage-price spiral, although not openly and explicitly. On December 5, 1955, the American Federation of Labor had merged with the CIO. On February 13, 1956, it called for a new round of "substantial" wage and welfare payment increases. The Eisenhower administration took no steps to halt the impending inflation in steel prices because it knew that the steel companies were prepared to accept wage increases and then raise prices. As a result, the nationwide steel strike which began on July 1, 1956 ended with acceptance of a wage rise of 45.6 cents an hour over the three-year period of the union contract and a rise in steel prices. In August, and again in October of 1956, the price index hit record highs, largely as a result of the rise in steel prices.

Despite inflationary pressures in the first four years of Eisenhower's administration, little use was made of the monetary policy which the Republicans had favored in the 1952 campaign. Paradoxically, the main effort to control inflation was along lines of fiscal policy. The budget was balanced in July 1956. Drastic cuts were made in military expenditures. So great were these that the administration was severely criticized by such prominent military figures as General Ridgway. The size of the armed forces was reduced, and claims were made that national defense rested primarily on nuclear weapons. Eventually alleged neglect of national defense became a campaign issue for the Democrats supporting Kennedy in 1960.

In his second term, President Eisenhower used monetary policy in reverse. A decline of business in 1957 and 1958 led to a series of reductions in the Federal Reserve rediscount rate until it reached two and a quarter percent in March 1958. This was one of a number of anti-recession moves which included an increase in expenditures by the

Post Office Department for purposes of modernization by $2 billion, greater FHA authorizations, elimination of interest on GI loans, an increase in the authorizations of the Export-Import Bank by $2 billion, and numerous pleas to consumers to buy more. By April 1958, however, the recession had become the worst in postwar history and unemployment reached almost seven million. Truman and others recommended that taxes be cut and defense expenditures increased, but the administration was unwilling to adopt such vigorous methods to speed recovery. By 1960, recovery was under way, and the problem of inflation had reappeared. A steel strike—the longest in history (July 15, 1959 to January 4, 1960)—had been settled by a further increase in wages and prices. Despite the long and substantial inflation, the President's Committee on Price Stability, headed by Vice-President Nixon, stated in 1960 that the threat of inflation had been averted.

In summary, inflation, a great new form of economic unbalance, focused and intensified the struggle for power in the administrations of Truman and Eisenhower. Neither President was very effective in coping with the resulting economic and political problems. President Truman understood clearly the ways in which inflation injured the small man, but he inherited no theoretical guide lines from the New Deal to enable him to deal with inflation. Worse yet, he had lost the political power that Roosevelt had, the Grand Alliance. The brain trust had long since been discarded as a political liability. With singular aversion to ideology, New Dealers avoided the theoretical development of their earlier beliefs. President Eisenhower was similarly ill-equipped to meet the problems of inflation, and during his administration a group of pro-inflation big businessmen all but captured the executive branch of the Federal Government.

But as we said at the beginning of this chapter, the history of the struggle over inflation in the days of Truman and

Eisenhower enables us to go further in developing the new socioeconomic theory needed to solve the American problem of power. This history reveals clearly (1) that neither Keynesianism nor countervailing power provide satisfactory answers for the power problems of an affluent inflationary society, and (2) that to explain the current situation in the United States, any new theoretical concepts must give some attention to the action of power groups in overwriting the price-wage fabric. Politics, sociology, and economics are interrelated. Without a theory of the political and social causes of concentrated power, we cannot have a realistic economic theory of concentrated power. In short, in addition to a new economics, we need a theory or science of power.

IX

The Science of Power

THE history of the power problem in the United States has passed through three distinct stages. In the beginning, the problem was essentially one of *group competition*. The rural population as a group fought the power and encroachment of the urban business interests as a group. After the Civil War, the destruction of individualism by economic concentration developed. The farmers, as individuals, feared the power of large corporations as monopolies. They thought it would damage them economically as individuals. They also feared the undemocratic control of big business over the Federal Government. In this concern, they were joined by the weak labor movement. The power problem had become a problem of protecting individuals and *individualism*. But with the Depression of 1929, the power struggle entered a third phase. The power problem became one of rectifying *economic unbalance* caused by concentrated power.

The problem of unbalance from concentration was not prepared for by the evolution of new economic theory. The indigenous beginnings in America of a national power economics in the work of Daniel Raymond and H. C. Carey were neglected by Americans, and British classicism became our orthodox economic theory. The departures from classicism by Keynes and Swedish economists were also largely ignored. Classical doctrine and its revisions, however, had no answer for the catastrophic unbalance created by the Depression of 1929. When the New Deal took over in 1933 under Franklin Roosevelt, it did so without the support of either a valid economics or a suitable social ideology. New Dealers also lacked a science of power. Their approach was largely pragmatic. Gradually they evolved a form of Keynesianism in deficit spending, and a political approach to the power problem in the concept of countervailing power. When the newer forms of unbalance due to concentrated power appeared after World War II—inflation and inflation depressions—Truman, Eisenhower, and Kennedy had no scientific answers. Both deficit spending and countervailing power failed to solve the problems of unbalance caused by inflation.

We Americans are too pragmatic and political. We need urgently an integrated political, economic and social ideology as the basis for government and business policy. We need leaders who will approach our problems scientifically rather than through pragmatism, compromise, or vague idealism. We should return to the Wilsonian type of leadership, which was not merely idealistic but was also scientifically oriented. Through theory, Wilson sought to discover the scientific basis of the general interest. In other words, we need leadership which follows (1) a new power sociology and (2) a new politico-economics based on a power economic model rather than the old classical no-power, free-enterprise economic model.

In this chapter, an attempt will be made to outline tentatively the bases of a science of power. The task is a big one. It cannot be accomplished fully here. In the following chapters we will also try to outline the major features of a new politico-economic model. Finally, on the basis of a proposed science of power and a new politico-economic model, we will discuss solutions for the current power problem.

THE NATURE OF POWER

Let us now raise some basic questions about power. What actually is the current nature of power in American society? How does our conception of power, viewed in the abstract, our theory of power, relate to our twentieth century society, structured around the super-institution, the great corporation? To what extent is the allocation of power in this corporate society justifiable on a rational or scientific basis? Some have insisted that in the eighteenth and early nineteenth centuries there was a rational basis for the allocation of power, and that the allocation changed and became irrational, irresponsible, and unprincipled with the decline of classical individualistic society and the emergence of corporate organic society. Power was centered in the older society in the laws of nature, and the social laws based on natural law. The state monopolized the instruments of power, but merely for the purpose of administering natural law or insuring its free operation.

In the transition to an organic society, power moved away from law and into institutions, which in turn concentrated power in the hands of the few individuals who controlled them. By what reason or social principle, then, did the power devolve upon these individuals? Specifically, why has much power been transferred from the free market to the top executives of the great corporations?

Power has been defined as the ability to achieve purposes and to force people to act in ways that reduce their independence. This ability was first acquired from the possession of *things* which other men needed, such as land or capital. But as economic life grew more complex, *things* became less important and *relationships* became increasingly important. With the rise of the organic corporate world, power was much more the possession of relationships in the organization of things than mere material possession. Thus power today is not very much a matter of wealth, and is mainly a matter of position, which can be defined as the possession of relationship rights over other people, who can be numbered sometimes in the millions.

The few men in our society who have power are able to attract and compel. Thus they possess two attributes of power. On the one hand, men come to them to obtain the privileges that they can dispense because their positions involve relationships with others. On the other hand, they can compel men to do what they wish by withholding. The corporate executive, for example, can attract by offering income, functions, and delegated power. He can also compel compliance by threatening denial of advantages upon which economic and social life depend. *Power in corporate society consists of a top position in an organic hierarchy,* whether it is the business corporation, a union, the military services, or the government. The nearer the position is to the top of the organism, the greater the power.

The moral philosophy behind this power delegation in a democratic society is that this kind of organic structure benefits the individual. Since democracy must be defined as the development of the potential of individuals, the "affirmation of their essence," there can be no other justification so long as democracy is accepted as socially fundamental. The allocation is not for the purpose of the welfare of the state, or of the corporate bodies, or of a corporate state conceived of as a synthesis of state and corporate bodies, or of a given class in society such as an aristocracy, theocracy, plutocracy, or a dictatorship of the proletariat. The allocation rests squarely on the welfare and growth of the individual. The rational basis of this allocation of power thus depends on the belief that the underlying reality of society consists of the lives of individuals and that their welfare is all that matters.

When one comes to the scientific basis for the allocation of power in modern organic society, various questions arise.

In the older classical period of freedom and free enterprise, power was taken away from individuals and lodged in the hands of the state, but the state followed the principle of laissez-faire. This, in effect, meant two things. (1) The state for the most part allowed individuals to pursue their own interests without interference. (2) When the state interfered, it did so only to enforce the laws of the government, based presumably on natural law. Power, in the last analysis, resided in law. When individuals followed supply and demand in economic life, they were submitting to natural law. When the state defended itself against external aggression and punished thieves within the domestic sphere, it was protecting private property or enforcing the natural law of property. This allocation of power in law rather than in men or in institutions, and in the state merely as an enforcer of law, was "scientific" in that society was considered as a complex of behavior based on natural law.

But is our current power allocation scientific, if we still consider the welfare of the individual as the ultimate end? The answer can be affirmative if the power allocation in organic corporate structures provides maximum efficiency in the satisfaction of individual needs and in providing for the maximum growth and freedom of the individual. Can one agree, however, that these *are* the results? Doubts have been voiced since the beginnings of our national history. They were expressed by Bryan, Wilson, Theodore Roosevelt, La Follette, Norris, Brandeis, and many others. Franklin Roosevelt, Truman, and Kennedy have been less concerned about this problem, but nevertheless, concerned. The concern expressed itself in Roosevelt's attack on the "economic royalists" and the return of Truman and Kennedy to the concept of the general interest.

If the allocation of power in corporate hierarchies required only productive efficiency for its justification, the great economic achievements of the last hundred years would amply justify it. But the concentration of power has reduced equality, which is the basis of freedom. Without freedom, the individual may have material prosperity, but he cannot fully grow and develop. In this way, power has threatened democracy as a social arrangement designed to foster individual maturity. Apart from damage to the individual, such a social organization may be "unscientific." Is a society which discards or limits individual motivation and the action of self-interest sound either socially or psychologically? Put another way, is there a mass mind, an organic or corporate soul, an "organization man," a state above the people, a material world without a spiritual world? More specifically, from the standpoint of economics, once we have discarded the classical laws of supply and demand and the free market price system as coordinating and directing factors in our economy, are there other laws of coordination which apply to a concentrated corporate power-structured economy which justify or guide this kind of economic organization? Are there adequate ways of protecting the freedom of the individual in such a society? Probably such laws exist, but they have not been thought out or consciously accepted. The concentrated corporate society has evolved and has functioned without a rationale. But it now reveals signs of malfunctioning, and even crisis, because of the absence of a scientific rationale which can give it guidance.

WHAT ARE POWER PROBLEMS OR THE POWER PROBLEM?

This is to say that there are problems of power or a basic power problem. Our society is a power-structured society. In the preceding pages, we have discussed in various ways the nature of power in American life and why it has caused problems. At this point, we will attempt to summarize.

Why is power a problem? It is a problem because (1) it adversely affects human motivation; (2) it becomes disastrously destructive; (3) it violates or negates freedom; (4) its operation results in malfunctioning and crisis; and (5) it causes social disorder, power struggles, and social unbalance.

The worst effects of the use of power are power motivation and destruction. Individuals who seek power in any social organization, whether it is the family, a community organization, a legislative body, or a business organization, are inclined first to ignore ethics, and second to subordinate other values or ideals to their desire for power. The individual seeking power becomes unethical. Power has a corrupting influence, since power is might, and it is all too easy for the person who has it to conclude that "might makes right." Power is a form of temptation. It requires a great deal of character for the person with power to subordinate its use to worthwhile goals which are unselfish, or, if selfish, are not injurious to others. Anyone who has participated in an organization of some kind can recall instances of disruption and injury when one or more individuals has become power-motivated and has sought personal power unscrupulously.

The most serious power problem of our time, however, is its destructive use. Destructive use of power ranges from the commonplace level of the mother who exercises her power over a helpless child to injure it psychologically, and sometimes even physically, to the horrible possibilities of hydrogen warfare. Both we and the Russians spend billions of dollars and exert scientific effort to the maximum to gain destructive power that would wipe out humanity in a few hours. Objectively viewed, it seems incredible that people, no matter what their social philosophy, can contemplate such a consequence, let alone bend every effort toward its accomplishment. This is our greatest overall social power problem. One hopeful possibility in the achievement of the highest level of destructive power is that no one may dare to use it.

A third power problem consists of the negation of freedom. At the outset, we outlined the conflict between power on the one hand and freedom and individual development on the other. Power reduces or destroys equality. Because individual development requires positive as well as negative freedom, inequality removes the opportunity needed for full development. With the growth of inequality, negative freedom was not fully capable of fostering individual growth. Thus society destroys freedom when it is structured in such a way as to seriously limit the growth potential of the individual. This is not sufficiently realized, and causes only mild concern because of ambivalence as to social values. Do we love freedom, or do we love bigness, material progress, and power?

But there is yet a fourth problem. We are concerned with goals other than freedom. In capitalism, we have sought greater production of goods and services, and economic efficiency and productivity through economic balance. Inherently, capitalism is a system of economic organization which provides economic balance, and through balance more effectively promotes productive efficiency. In the past, the balance of supply and demand, and price and cost, promoted efficiency. But the concentration of power in business and labor increasingly destroyed balance. Without a general balancing factor, modern *power-structured capitalism* experiences depression and inflation and even low rates of production growth. The results are loss of potential production and even crisis. Thus a serious power problem arises because the capitalist goal of balance is violated. It is curious that American capitalism, through power-structuring, strikes at economic balance, the very foundation of capitalism. Business concentration has destroyed the free market, but no alternative balancing factor has been provided.

Thus in contravening one of the basic values or goals of capitalism, malfunctioning and crisis, through lack of balancing, develop. If one looks deeper, however, it is evident that *when power causes malfunctioning, it must be because those who have it violate the scientific relations underlying the existing social organization. Power leads to economic unbalance because the use of power violates economic theory.* In 1929, our economic system had already to a large degree abandoned the balancing factor of the free market. When the Great Depression came, those in power who had destroyed the free market system sat waiting for it to pull them out of the depression. First, they had violated the economics which they professed, and then they insisted that this rejected economics would restore prosperity. When the public demanded the use of a new economics, Keynesianism, they violently opposed its use despite its obvious effectiveness and the obsolescence of the old economics.

The tendency of power to cause crisis and malfunctioning when unchecked is due to the fact that those in power have an extreme interest in the *status quo.* Whether it be in ancient Egypt or in modern America, they accept traditionalism as a defense mechanism against change and the resulting loss of power. But social organization and its underlying technology change, and traditional beliefs and principles become inapplicable. Traditionalism may retard change, but, most serious, *it also causes the persistent application of unsuitable theory or "science" to the solution of social problems.* The time comes when this process, instead of preventing change, may cause crises and violent change. At this point, those in power must either relinquish their power or adopt new beliefs. After the advent of the great depression, business lost power for these reasons. To regain power they had to accept Keynesianism and give up belief in laissez-faire. They could not hold power in a badly functioning economic system, *and to restore function and balance they had to accept a new economics.*

But Keynesianism, which saved American capitalism, was the solution of non-business groups. Businessmen grudgingly accepted it. They sought, under Eisenhower, to limit its use. No effective control over inflation was established. Eisenhower even proposed the elimination of the Council of Economic Advisers, the administrative reflection of Keynesianism in the Federal Government. In other words, having regained power, they sought to retreat from the newer theory and to limit its use. But more serious, the newer theory was not enough to replace the balance of the free market. Instead of retreat, there was need for advance toward a broader theoretical basis for balance in a concentrated economic system. Keynesianism had its limitations because of the up-writing of the price-wage fabric. The time had come for theory which would provide for greater centralization in the control of the economy, and more comprehensive control than control of the income flow or the substitution of group for individual competition. The time had come also for a new economic model which highlighted the role of the great corporation in American society, and a new power economics based on it.

A fifth type of power problem consists of the social disorder, struggle, and social unbalance it often creates. Where there are two kinds of coincidence, that between social structure and philosophy and that between power in different fields, this type of power problem does not arise. For example, there was little general struggle for power in the Middle Ages, if we exclude power struggles among the members of the power élite, the leading nobles, kings, and clergy. Society was hierarchical and the philosophy of life justified the hierarchy. There was acceptance of personal power, classes, immobility between classes, inequality, tradition, conformity, lack of change, price-fixing, and planning. Social structure, theory, codes of behavior, and ideals were integrated. Only after disintegration began in both structure and belief was there a struggle for power. The coincidence between structure and philosophy had been broken by the rise of individualism. Great social disorder followed until, under individualistic classical society, a new coincidence was reached. The economic and political systems were no longer hierarchical. Belief and structure agreed. The resulting beliefs and social order involved no personal power, no inequality, and no classes.

Lack of coincidence may occur in different fields or aspects of social life. In modern American life there is a sharp cleavage between economics and political life. Economic life is hierarchical and political life is democratic. Put in an extreme way, the nation is half-slave and half-free. Even within such a field as race relations, part of society may not suffer from discrimination, but for other parts, discrimination may be acute. There is little remaining discrimination, for example, against Irish Catholics and Jews, but much discrimination against Negroes and Puerto Ricans. The lack of coincidence causes the latter groups to stage a bitter struggle for power in race relations. Similar disparities may be found among religious and other social groupings. But the main disparity is between our political and economic life. It has led to a number of great power struggles in American history.

The lack of integration in our culture creates our power problems. At any given period in history the groups having power can govern in ways which cause malfunctioning, crisis, or unfairness. This is due to a lack of social integration in that philosophy and social integration are throughout or in part inconsistent. The crises, malfunctioning, or unfairness create motives for a power struggle. The lack of social integration creates the possibility of a struggle. When the struggle occurs, we have a power problem consisting of a struggle for power of major importance due to some form of social malfunctioning. This is a workable hypothesis for the cause of power problems. With this tentative hypothesis of causation, we can proceed to an analysis of the structure of power in present-day American society. Both cause and structure may provide a comprehensive theory of power.

THE STRUCTURE OF POWER

It will be generally admitted that we do not live in an equalitarian society in the sense that all men have equal or near equal economic, political or social power. Perhaps no such society has ever existed, but early America more nearly approximated it than the America of today. After the Civil War, with the rise of industrialism and the large corporation, power of all kinds became increasingly concentrated in fewer hands. The question is not whether there is concentrated power in American life, but what the extent and nature of it is. We can conceive of American society as moderately concentrated with considerable power in the hand of a public consisting largely of independent and thoughtful individuals. Or we can regard the concentration as more extreme, with little or no power in the hands of the ordinary man. It is our belief that the structure of power in the United States today more nearly resembles the latter construct than the former.

A structural model of current America was provided by C. Wright Mills in his book, *The Power Élite*. The model is an exaggerated one of acute concentration of power. In it, the public, or rather the masses, have very little if any power. Representative of this view are Mills' statements that ". . . the powers of ordinary men are circumscribed by the everyday worlds in which they live . . . the very framework of modern society confines them to projects not their own." Ordinary men "feel that they are without purpose in an epoch in which they are without power." [1] They do not create their occupations; they cannot regard themselves as superior in any way because they are part of a broad lower base, below which are only derelicts and social misfits; and they make no decisions of any consequence.

Above the broad base of the public or masses, Mills finds

1 Mills, C. Wright, *The Power Élite*, p. 3

a "middle level of power." On this level are politicians, pressure groups, and various celebrities. In his opinion, Congress does not make the crucial decisions, and congressmen are mere implementers of major decisions, and brokers in the determination of issues of secondary importance as between competing interest groups. In this middle level also are religious, educational, and social organizations. Instead of having a status of independent power, these organizations are regarded by Mills as "decentralized areas" which are increasingly shaped by the higher circles of power.

At the apex of the hierarchy of power in the Mills model is the *power élite*. It consists of a small group of men who have attained power through their control of large corporations or large military bodies, or because they belong to the "political directorate," the top fifty or sixty men administering the Federal Government. As the three domains of power, the large corporation, the military, and the Federal Government, become enlarged and more centralized, the power of the élite is greatly enhanced, and their relationships with each other increase. Power is acquired only insofar as persons have strategic positions within those three major domains. The power élite, holding the strategic command posts, can create jobs, look down on others, and make decisions of major consequence.

Mills regards the members of the power élite as a "more or less compact social and psychological entity; they have become self-conscious members of a social class . . . they come readily to define themselves as inherently worthy of what they possess; they come to believe themselves 'naturally élite.' " [1] To call the power élite an upper class, however, involves a rather broad use of the concept of class. Class usually denotes little movement into or out of a social group and the group Mills describes may have too much social mobility to

[1] *Ibid.*, pp. 11-14

be considered a class. Some also regard a class as a body which is largely perpetuated through heredity.

THE THEORY OF BALANCE REJECTED

Democratic conceptions of American society seldom were so unrealistic as to rule out the presence of some difference in the degrees of power held by individuals. However, it was assumed that individuals generally were not only equal before the law and in their capacity to determine elections, but in their economic and social power as well. They were also rational and open to persuasion from any quarter. Public issues were discussed freely, the pros and cons weighed, and public opinion openly reached. On the basis of discussion, broad issues arose which represented the interests of large groups. Countering groups would appear, and the differences decided in elections or in legislative bodies. Congress and state legislatures were visualized as balancing agencies and arenas where conflicting interests met and agreement was reached by a process of compromise. The executive branch of government was subordinate to the legislative branch, and administered legislative decisions on policy. Executives were not the policy makers.

Mills, going to extremes, discards this conception of government as totally unreal in present-day America. He says that "Americans cling to the idea that the government is a sort of automatic machine, regulated by the balancing of competing interests. This image of politics is simply a carry-over from the official image of the economy." [1] In other words, government is thought to function in the manner of the competitive free market. In the competitive model of the market, the forces of demand and supply meet and are balanced at an equilibrium price where supply and demand are equal. A "compromise" is reached through prices between the wishes of sellers who would all like to sell at a high price,

[1] *Ibid.,* p. 242

and buyers who want to buy as cheaply as possible. The free market, however, declines and disappears as some buyers or sellers obtain monopolistic market power. In like manner, it is assumed that if the few people of the power élite obtain great economic power, the important political decisions are not made in Congress through a balancing or debating process. This "romantic pluralism" where interests outside the government are represented in Congress and their powers offset and balanced against those of other interests is, according to Mills, a picture of the middle levels of power. This amounts to saying that the power élite, and not the voting public, make the really important policy decisions in our society.

The picture of a balanced political society has its origins in the philosophy and the nascent political science of the eighteenth century. Society was visualized as a collection of individuals who expressed their will in atomistic competition with millions of other individuals. The ideals implicit in the individual competition were (1) a balance or harmony of interests, (2) behavior according to natural law, and (3) the expression of the general interest, or the good of the whole society. As a result, the rich would not exploit the poor, or one economic interest, such as agriculture, take advantage of manufacturing and trade. It was a checks-and-balances society.

THE NATURE OF THE POWER ÉLITE

If, as Mills contends, there is a power élite, the composition of the élite is of paramount importance. Who are these men? What is their background? What are their interests and policies? What are their goals for the United States? Mills answers the first two of these questions, but gives us little on the third and fourth.

In the description of the élite, Mills begins with local society. In early America, and even until the Civil War, local society had great influence. The early élite consisted largely of a collection of local élites. A local élite still exists consisting of the bankers, prominent businessmen, and the wealthy of the towns and smaller cities of the United States. These "local upper classes ... make up the social backbone of the Republican party." [1] They form a small right wing in American politics with their major object the destruction of the achievements of the New Deal and the Fair Deal.

The local upper classes, Mills believes, are of minor importance. Their power and status are increasingly challenged by (1) the use of smaller communities by commuters from metropolitan centers, and (2) the entry of branches of large corporations into their areas. The commuting population distracts and challenges the local élite, and the executives of corporation branches demand local recognition.

The American élite is thus essentially metropolitan. Before the Civil War a metropolitan élite had developed which was compact and stable. Together with representatives of the local élite, it exercised great influence over both state and federal governments. It consisted of the chief members of the older wealthy families. An attempt was made to make it a pedigreed upper class. But the power of money was too great. New fortunes were acquired in railroads, commerce, manufacturing and banking. The "nouveaux riches" knocked insistently at the doors of the older landed rich and had to be admitted. Mrs. Astor agreed to associate with Mrs. Vanderbilt. The upper class thus became a group of the wealthiest people without pedigree or fixed membership, but it was nationally recognized, homogeneous, and had a strong sense of unity. It belonged to the best clubs. It sent its children to the best private schools and the Ivy League colleges, especially Harvard and Yale. Uniformity of dress, manners, and attitude developed. It came to be called the "Metropolitan Four Hun-

[1] *Ibid.*, p. 35

dred" as a result of Ward McAllister's listings, and in more recent years it has been listed in the *Social Register*.

This part of the upper class aspired to the role of top decision making. Some of its members have reached this goal and are part of the power élite. But the Four Hundred, according to Mills, are not the power élite *per se*. The significance of this lies in the fact that wealth as such does not guarantee top power in our society. It is, of course, an important means of obtaining it. But American society is not a hierarchy presided over by the wealthiest families. A few Latin American, Asian, and African countries reveal this pattern. They are oligarchies of wealth, but largely because of the predominance of agriculture in their economic life. The industrialization of the United States and the growth of large corporations reduced the power of the Four Hundred. The executive of the large corporation challenged the power of the wealthy families, and the development of mass media of publicity challenged their social status.

The very rich, if they wish to be active, are usually part of the power élite. But they are not alone in their power. They share it with corporate executives, the top of the military hierarchy, and the chief government executives. They hold power not so much because they are very rich, but because they are part of what Mills calls the Corporate Rich. Their power is not due to wealth alone. It arises because wealth is in the form of securities which give them control over large corporations. Since corporations are our most powerful institutions, control of them gives great power.

THE CORPORATE RICH

The Corporate Rich, which, according to Mills, is the most important part of the power élite, consists of some very rich men, but mainly of the chief executives who rise to the top of their organizations because of promotion in the corporate hierarchy.[1] The chief executives are the largest and most powerful part of the Corporate Rich. Mills regards them as the most powerful men in American society, surpassing even the President and the top military men.

If the Corporate Rich obtain their power primarily by rising within the hierarchy of the large corporation, it may be concluded that the most important members of the power élite select themselves.[2] There is a desire to perpetuate the corporation by choosing men who are similar to those in power. These men are alike in personal traits, background, training, and beliefs and attitudes. One rises to the top first by becoming like those at the top, and then by obtaining their acceptance. One comes from the middle class, is Protestant, and graduates from an Ivy League college. Managerial ability or training in a school of business are not of primary importance. Of more significance are the personal traits of character, judgment, ability to fit in, ability to lead, ability to conduct problem-solving meetings, tolerance, nonintellectualism, and caution.

The economic power of the Corporate Rich is varied and comprehensive. It consists of power (1) to determine the kind and quality of products and thus determine the nature of the consumption enjoyed by the general public; (2) to determine the volume of production and the amount of consumption; (3) to determine the rate of growth of production and our ultimate standard of living; (4) to determine in part the distribution of income as between owners of capital and labor and as between different kinds of labor; and (5) to play a significant part in the relative allocation of production between (a) public and private consumption, (b) capital and consumers goods, (c) military and civilian production, and

1 *Ibid.*, p. 148. As Mills puts it, "The corporate rich thus includes members of the big city rich, of the Metropolitan 400, of the national rich who possess the great American fortunes, as well as the chief executives of the major corporations."

2 Ibid., p. 319. The men "in the same circles choose one another."

(d) the kinds of military production. Looked at from the viewpoint of Mills, their power in all these respects is extreme. Although one may not accept such an extreme view, it must be admitted that those who control our great corporations have very substantial power in all these areas.

The power of the corporate rich obtained from the control of large corporations is very great. But of even greater significance is the power gained from governmental infiltration. Big business lost control of the Federal Government as a result of the Great Depression and the advent of Franklin Roosevelt. During the administrations of Coolidge and Hoover, they had exercised great influence in Washington, largely from the outside, through lobbies or through personal associations with Congressmen. Such power as they had was not exerted from *within* the government. With Roosevelt, the power of big business was severely curtailed, and during the years 1933-1939, business mounted a vigorous attack on the government, hoping that the New Deal could be defeated at the polls, but they were unsuccessful. By 1940, however, big business had begun to accept many aspects of the New Deal as inevitable. Social security, collective bargaining, the farm program, and the unbalanced budget were the new order of the day. It was decided that business should go along with much of the New Deal, cease bitter opposition to the administration, and seek to join the administration through service in top administrative positions. A golden opportunity to do this had appeared in the form of World War II.

The war required colossal industrial effort which in turn required great collaboration between government and big business. Civil servants, college professors, and lawyers were not able to administer this joint effort between government and business. They did not have sufficient knowledge and they could not implement their decisions. As a result, the representatives of big business entered the Federal Government at points of great power in the administrative agencies.

They controlled the use of scarce raw materials and the production goals from *within* the government. When the war ended, they remained *within* the government.

It might have been expected that the infiltration of the Federal Government by big business would have been reduced or eliminated after World War II as it had been after World War I. But this was not the case because we had entered a new era in which huge military expenditures were to become a permanent peacetime phenomenon. The collaboration of business and government had to continue on a large scale, and the economy was vitally affected by the volume and orientation of defense expenditures. Thus business continued to exercise great control over the government, but from *within* and *through* the administration rather than through lobbies or legislation.

The Eisenhower administration was notable in the degree to which businessmen controlled the important positions in the administrative hierarchy. Of fifty-three men regarded as the chief federal decision-makers, thirty were connected in some way with the world of the large corporation. The leading executives under Eisenhower were conscious of the high degree of business control and some of them were inclined to justify it openly. For example, Douglas McKay, Secretary of the Interior, stated in a speech that "we're here in the saddle in an administration representing business and industry." [1] Then one can also cite the celebrated statement of Defense Secretary Charles Wilson that the interests of General Motors *are* the interests of the United States. Another typical statement was that of J. K. Jessup that "Any president who wants to run a prosperous country depends on the corporation at least as much as—probably more than—the corporation depends on him." [2] As chairman of the Board of *Fortune*

[1] Speech before the Chamber of Commerce, April 29, 1953, quoted in Mills, *op. cit.,* p. 168

[2] Mills, *op. cit.,* p. 169

Magazine, he visualized the large corporation as having assumed the responsibility of making the country run efficiently both economically and politically.

THE WARLORDS AND THE MILITARY ASCENDANCY

A second element in the power élite, according to Mills, consists of the top military men, the heads of the military hierarchy and its vast administrative bureaucracy. Since World War II, leading military men and their underlying organizations have become more rather than less powerful. Throughout the nineteenth century and until World War II, civilians dominated the military. A trend in the reverse direction is now occurring, in which military interests are increasingly affecting and in some cases dominating civilian life. As military power increases, the prestige of military men and their role in government are also increasing.

In the United States especially, the military had occupied a subordinate position. We were relatively isolated and were not threatened with invasion. The heroes of American life were not so much the generals of the army as the generals of business and finance. Moreover, we insisted that the military were the servants of civilians, and in some quarters, the assumption of the Presidency by a general was regarded as against the public interest. The Second World War has made great changes in our attitudes.

The reason for the civilian power held by the military is the effect of military preparedness on the economy. Some, like Arthur Krock, have gone as far as to assert that our economy is linked to war. Because it is essentially a war economy, a drastic decline in international tensions resulting in a great decrease in defense expenditures could prove disastrous unless substitute forms of production and expenditures can be found. Defense expenditures account for one-half to two-thirds of federal expenditures. The large proportions of the military aspects of the economy have led to the merger of the huge military bureaucracy with the corporate bureaucracy. During World War II, parts of these bureaucracies were interchangeable. At times a man was a corporative executive, at others an administrator in the War Production Board or in the Defense Department, and at still others an officer in uniform.

As military men have gained power, they have (1) become more political, (2) entered the administration and policy determination of non-military or only indirectly military affairs, and (3) accepted administrative positions in large corporations. In their "politicalization" the top military have sought by political means to protect and advance their rising power and social status. They have large vested interests to defend. They have also been appointed or elected to high civilian posts including the presidency. Examples of this are the careers of Generals Eisenhower, Marshall, Clark, Smith, and Clay. Most of the leading military men have entered into debates over public policy. Noteworthy in this respect are Marshall, Bradley, MacArthur, Wedemeyer, and Rickover, in addition to General Eisenhower. Their great influence has spread beyond military affairs into governmental and corporate life. They have a vital influence on foreign policy. Congress defers to military opinion, accepting most of their proposals almost without question.

THE POLITICAL DIRECTORATE

A third element in Mills' picture of the power élite is the group of leading administrators in the Federal Government which Mills calls the political directorate. These men consist of the President and Vice-President and the members of the Cabinet, the undersecretaries and chief officers of the departments, the "sub-Cabinet" or Executive Office of the President which includes such men as the Director of the Budget, the Director of the Office of Defense Mobilization, and the White House staff which includes assistants to the President, the

President's personal secretary, and the press secretary. Depending on how inclusive one wishes to be, this group numbers from fifty to two hundred persons.

Those who hold these positions are not for the most part professional politicians. They have not entered these posts after a long service in Congress or in state governments. In the Eisenhower group only the Vice-President and the Attorney General could be regarded as party politicians. The group also includes very few men who have risen in the ranks of the federal bureaucracy. In our American governmental system, cabinet or top executive positions are very rarely filled by division or bureau heads. Rise in the civil service stops at these ranks. Having reached this point, men are reluctant to give up civil service status for the higher, less secure, political executive positions. Moreover, they are seldom asked to fill these posts. Even in the State Department, the Secretary and Undersecretary are almost never career men.

It must be concluded, therefore, that the political directorate consists largely of "outsiders." Since they are outsiders, they have no common background or characteristics apart from those of the corporate rich and the military from which they are usually chosen. They do not have the characteristics of party politicians or of the political bureaucracy they administer. There are also no rules by which they are selected. Presumably their selection is largely determined by the President, but the selection of cabinets and other parts of the administration vary with different chief executives. The choice of Presidents themselves follows no strict set of rules apart from those of nominating conventions. By the time these meet, the major part of the selection has usually occurred, since only three or four men have any real chance of nomination.

THE WEAKNESSES OF THE MILLS MODEL

Not all agree with Mills that the political power of the ordinary man has become negligible and that the concentration of power in corporations and in the military coalesces in the political directorate to create a pinnacle of American economic and political power. They are not agreed also that the power of Congress is confined only to local or minor national affairs.

One must conclude that although the concentration of power described by Mills is substantially correct as to the *nature* of the concentration, it exaggerates the *degree* of it. Voluntary associations, lobbies, and unions are still significant power factors. With three-quarters of the newspapers against him, Truman still obtained a victory over Dewey in 1948. The public is not entirely molded by mass media unless a form of totalitarianism is established. The power élite in America does not head a fascist state.

But granted the weaknesses of the Mills model, there are many elements of truth in it as a description of the structure of power in American life. More and more power has gravitated into the hands of a few corporate executives. These men obtain positions of power for the most part not because of their wealth, but because they are selected from the ranks by the men already in power. The corporate élite, or power group, at times enters into and exercises great control over the executive branch of the Federal Government. The executive branch steadily gains predominance in power over the Congress. Military men and professional politicians share power in the executive branch with the corporate élite.

Thus, in a rough outline form, we have now reached the beginnings of a comprehensive model or theory of power. Power problems are due to social disintegration in which the social and economic theory of those in power becomes inconsistent with the needs and structure of society. The struc-

)f society is currently one of power concentrated in / or four hierarchies of institutions. Mills includes only corporation, the military, and the executive branch of the Federal Government. Labor unions should be added. The top men in these four areas are more responsible for the basic decisions made in the United States than is Congress or the average voter. But it is an exaggeration to call them an élite since a true élite involves selection on the basis of birth, merit, or some one selection factor rigorously adhered to. American life is too flexible and mobile to permit the formation of a true élite. Nevertheless, the top men in these four areas exercise the primary role of policy determination in our country and at times the top of the executive branch of the Federal Government consists almost exclusively of these men.

This tentative theory or model of power, when combined with a new, power-oriented economics, can, through synthesis, give us a comprehensive new socio-politico-economic model or theory. As we have repeatedly said, we need such a theory to provide a scientific basis for the solution of our current American power problem. An attempt at such a synthesis is made in the succeeding chapter.

X

The Socio-Politico-Economic Society

An integrated picture of modern American life must be drawn in terms of a whole which is not divided into separate social, economic, and political parts. In reality, a culture is not a mere collection of the viewpoints gained from studying the different social sciences. It consists of (1) a technological base or substructure, (2) an institutional superstructure with a center and a periphery, (3) a system of control, (4) a set of aims or goals, and (5) a psychological composite of beliefs, theories, ethics, customs, morals, attitudes, and general philosophy. In our attempt to describe a new model or theory of our modern concentrated power society, we shall briefly deal with these five basic elements of culture.

THE SUBSTRUCTURE

At the base of modern society is current technology. Beginning with the technical and industrial changes which occurred after 1750 in England, and in other western nations at a somewhat later date, we have evolved a complex modern technical substructure which is partly mechanical and partly chemical and electrical. It is now advancing into an atomic phase. On the basis of these technical changes, there have followed economic institutional changes which may be briefly listed: the separation of labor from capital; the factory system; the use of nonhuman power, machinery, and equipment in production; the growth of transportation; the growth of mass communication, the increase of speed in production, communication, and transportation; the rapid advance in the volume and variety of production; the growth in the size of production units, or large-scalism; urbanism; and the growth of specialization by task, occupation, and area.

THE SUPERSTRUCTURE

Accompanying the essentially technical-institutional changes were changes resulting from and assisting the accumulation of capital and providing a legal basis for the management of large enterprises. The primary social instrument effecting these changes is the large corporation, which has become the dominant institution of our time. The corporation enabled large masses of capital to be invested in productive enterprises through dividing ownership rights into transferable shares. Through the election of managers and boards of directors, large numbers of owners could delegate their managerial rights to corporate executives. Without this delegation, large enterprises could not have been managed, since no organization can be operated by the direct managerial participation of thousands of owners. The corporation enabled a few experienced and trained persons to control the employment of millions of dollars of capital.

But the corporation did more than provide a means of huge capital accumulation and centralization of management. It established (1) a new system of property rights; (2) a new system of functional relationships among owners, managers, consumers, workers, the community, and the government; and (3) a means of centralizing the control of separate industries and of the economy as a whole. It became the focal point for the determination of political policies, for establishing living standards and goals, and for the creation of consumer wants. In fact, the large corporation is the center around which most of our politico-economic life revolves. The corporation is a superinstitution which exists within the state, but exercises a predominant control over the state through a process of politico-economic integration. *The center of modern American society is the large corporation.*

The periphery of which the large corporations in vital industries constitute the center is a variegated pattern of enterprise with lesser degrees of concentration and scale and with lesser economic importance. In terms of national income, about seven percent of our economic life is agricultural. There are 4.7 million farms, but only 2.2 million are commercial in that they are producing for a market. In agriculture, scale is generally small except in cattle raising and a few other fields. Concentration of control is virtually nonexistent. Economic coordination is achieved through the federal argricultural programs which convert farming into a politico-economic system. Some slight coordination is also achieved through cooperative marketing in fruit and dairy products. In the periphery also are parts of our manufacturing and most of our service and trade enterprises.

Fields of low concentration in manufacturing in which the large corporation is not dominant are bread and bakery products, luggage, machine shops, brick and hollow tile, commercial printing, men's and boys' suits, handbags and purses, women's and children's underwear, women's suits, dresses, and coats, fur goods, sawmills and planing mills, and many miscellaneous fields such as costume jewelry. In these fields the scale of production is also small. Large corporations dominate the utilities and transportation, as well as the steel, automobile, aluminum, electric lamp, locomotive, cigarette, typewriter, soap, corn products, sewing machine, and tire industries. In the middle ranges of concentration are industries such as cement.

In the periphery there are about two million retailers and

about three hundred thousand wholesalers. The vast majority of retailers are small in scale and lacking in market concentration. Through price discrimination laws, they have some connection with the legislative structure of the country, but they are less subject to political action than large corporations or farmers. Similar in economic organization are the 800,000 service businesses. Some of these are organized in chains, but for the most part they are small-scale, and there is little concentration. They are also unconnected with government except through regulations concerning the character and standards of their services. The general character of both retailing and service is affected by the centralizing influence upon them of the large manufacturing corporations. Finally, the periphery consists also of about 500,000 contract construction businesses and 600,000 miscellaneous businesses. Contractors are politico-economic to the extent that building is subject to numerous regulations, and much of it depends upon government spending.

It is uncertain where government enterprise and employment should be placed. Is it a part of the periphery around the large corporations, or is it an independent and equally important or even dominant area of our economic life? Government, including the armed forces, employs over 10,000,-000 people, or one-seventh of our labor force. To a large extent its functions and services, such as education and police and fire protection, are only indirectly related to economic processes. But its defense functions, which account for a very large part of government employment and expenditures, are closely connected with the activities of big business, and both determine and are determined by these activities. In this respect, government is not peripheral, but central to the economy. The classification of government as central depends on the nature of the control of the defense activity. If we assume that it is controlled through the influence of large corporations on the top levels of the federal administration, we must regard it as peripheral to these corporations. If control flows in the opposite direction, government is in a central position. Since the nature of government today reveals great business control in these areas, it is concluded that in the current corporate society government is to some extent peripheral.

Of ambiguous status also are the large unions. By 1958, union membership exceeded 18,000,000. The teamsters had 1,600,000 members; the auto workers, 1,280,000 and the steel workers, 1,020,000. Although unions are not industries and do not fit into our classification of industrial structure, they are important control bodies cutting across the structure and exercising considerable economic power. Insofar as they are able to exercise countervailing power against the large corporations, they can be regarded as having a central position in society. When they collaborate with corporations in raising prices or determining output they are sharing power with the large corporations or being dominated by them. In this respect, they are similar to government. When the latter offsets, directs, or regulates big business, it is in a central position. When it is controlled or dominated by big business, it is in a secondary position and its activities can be regarded as peripheral. Perhaps it should be concluded that both organized labor and government are largely peripheral, but that at times they assume a central role. Government assumes an important role in war, and also when it attempts to control the overall volume and flow of money purchasing power through fiscal or other policies to prevent depressions or curb inflation.

THE SYSTEM OF CONTROL

The term concentration has been defined by economists in various ways. For the most part, it has been used to mean a large share of the market. For example, if four large rubber companies account for ninety percent of the sales of rubber goods and tires, there is great concentration. If, on the other hand, a thousand companies accounted for ninety percent of the sales, there would be little concentration. If a thousand businesses were ninety percent of the businesses, there would be no concentration at all. But the large concentration we find in some fields of American business usually exhibits two other kinds of concentration in addition to control of a large share of the market. There are also (1) concentration of power over prices and output by a few firms, and (2) the control of these firms internally by a few people.

From the standpoint of market price the American economy is a great spectrum of price gradation ranging from purely competitive prices in a few commodities or securities, where no one seller has any market power, through a middle area where there is some price control and some market power, to a large area where there is a high degree of price control and market power. Businesses having this power are called monopolies when they have it exclusively, and oligopolies when they share it with a few other businesses. The price-market spectrum is skewed toward oligopoly. In terms of the value of the products sold, the American market is at least fifty percent oligopolistic.[1] Another thirty percent reveals imperfect or partial price control, and the remainder is either under government price control or competitive. Less than ten percent of the American price system can be regarded as strictly competitive.

The controls of the large corporation ramify through the economic system. Not only does General Motors control a large share of the automobile market; it controls thousands of auto dealers, exerts its influence on tire and parts manufacturers, strongly affects the sale of gasoline, of accessories,

[1] Forty-five percent of the industrial assets of the United States are owned by 135 corporations. *Cf.* Berle, Adolf, Jr., *The Twentieth Century Capitalist Revolution*, pp. 25-26. Berle asserts that seventy percent of the economy is controlled by the large corporations.

and of used cars, and exercises influence on all businesses by affecting the costs of transportation, the location of workers, and the volume of purchasing power. Everyone's income would be curtailed if the large automobile companies were to shut down. A protracted strike in this field can cause a recession. Also having great ramifying effect are the policies of the United States Steel Company. Not only do they affect employment and purchasing power in other industries, but they determine a part of the cost of doing business in many fields of manufacturing, transportation, the utilities, and construction.

Even though a large part of the American economy is still small-scale and to some extent competitive, it cannot be regarded as totally free enterprise. Controls and influence impinge on these relatively free businesses either from the government through regulation and through tax policies, or from large corporations which affect costs, purchasing power, the price at which goods can be sold at retail, and the manner of sale. Thousands of retailers, automobile dealers, subcontractors, and service industries are influenced or controlled by large corporations. They are in effect appendages of these larger bodies. Thus the economy is largely a pyramid with the great corporations and the government at the top, radiating control and power downward to a broad base consisting of small businesses, retailers, service businesses, and farmers. As Berle says, "The mid-twentieth century American capitalist system depends on and revolves around the operations of a relatively few very large corporations." [1]

Within the large corporation there is also concentration of power. Through the use of the proxy system, large corporations like the American Telephone and Telegraph Company, with over two million stockholders, are controlled by a management which, in effect, elects itself to power or selects its successors. About forty percent of the largest corporations

[1] Berle, *op. cit.*, p. 28

are controlled by management in this way. The remainder of the large corporations are controlled by minorities of the owners, sometimes holding as little as two percent of the voting stock. Only about six percent of the large corporations are controlled through a majority vote of the stock. In these cases, the majority of the stock is usually owned by a wealthy family, a group of wealthy families, or a combination of a wealthy family and a corporation. The majority, in the sense of the majority of a million stockholders, never controls. Large corporations are always controlled by minorities or by the management, except where very wealthy interests constitute a majority.

On top of the concentrated economic structure there is, as we have seen from reviewing Mills' theory of the élite, a concentrated political structure. The power of the Federal Government has grown in the last fifty years. Within the Federal Government, the executive power has grown. Although political power may not be wholly concentrated in the top federal administrators, much power is concentrated there. High policy decisions are often made by these men rather than by Congress. Although Congress is not always relegated to the "middle levels" of power, as Mills contends, its power is not as great as that of the Executive Branch. But at times it thwarts and checks the President in his attempts to lead in the determination of policy.

As to the composition of the "political directorate" and as to the role of the top military men in policy decisions, Mills' description again is valid except in the exaggeration of the degree to which big business always and inevitably absorbs all the key positions. In the Kennedy Administration, the role of big business in the higher circles was less than it was under Eisenhower. Although the three highest posts of the Secretaries of State, Treasury, and Defense, were filled by two businessmen and one head of a business-financed foundation, their views have not been altogether agreeable to big business. The Attorney General was the president's brother, and the first Secretary of Labor under Kennedy was not from the field of management, but a labor lawyer. The tendencies of the early New Deal were revived by the employment of college professors as top advisers and ambassadors. The higher circles still reflect the power of big business, but not to the extreme degree postulated by Mills. Nor does the top military seem to be in a position to determine domestic or even military policy to the extent that it could do so under Truman and Eisenhower.

THE GOALS

Professor Galbraith sees our concentrated corporate society as one of abundance which is dangerously preoccupied with production. It unbalances itself through inflation and the diversion of production from social to material investment. But we should not exaggerate our abundance. Although we overemphasize production and create social unbalance, our economy still suffers from much poverty in terms of our accepted standards of living. In 1957, eight percent of the spending units in the United States had money incomes of less than $1,000 a year, twenty-one percent had less than $2,000, and thirty-two percent, or almost a third, had less than $3,000. Not all spending units are families, but most of them are. A family income of less than $3,000 in 1957 was a very low income. At least $4,000 was needed for minimum comfort. We are a long way from the level at which we can begin to minimize production. Our problems are still not so much that we have reached an economy of abundance and are overemphasizing production, as that we have yet to increase money incomes in proportion to increased productivity.

Perhaps the crucial point to emphasize is that we have reached the stage in our development where a greater degree of centralized direction in the economy is not only needed but has become possible due to the concentration of economic control. Yet coordination and central planning are avoided because they are feared as violations of capitalist principles and because some groups benefit from unbalance. A better understanding of the kind of corporate capitalism in which we live might make us realize that a larger degree of economic coordination may not run counter to modern capitalism.

Although production may be the major goal of modern American capitalism, it is by no means the only goal, and we can distort the picture of capitalism by overemphasizing the production goal. For years, other goals have played their part. The goals are not only (1) production, but (2) efficiency, (3) security, (4) shorter hours and greater leisure, (5) full employment, (6) greater equality of income and wealth, and (7) some sort of economic and social balance. To be sure, in the last thirty-five years we have emphasized production, security, and employment, while leisure and equality have been given less consideration. But there is now a great rise in concern for shorter hours with the growing threat of automation, and although concern over "inequality and poverty" has been dormant, it is by no means dead and is now reviving in the so-called war on poverty.

The original basis of capitalism and the underlying basic need is balance. Capitalism began as a market price system where balance and allocation of resources were attained through competitive pricing. The free market has declined and all but disappeared. No wholly satisfactory substitute for the market as balancer, allocator, and central coordinator of the economy has been found. There is group competition or countervailing power which may promote balance to a slight extent. In addition, the Keynesian control of income flow through government plays a part in restoring and maintaining the flow of purchasing power as productivity increases. Without it, capitalism would have collapsed, once monopolistic tendencies had destroyed the income-balancing influence of the free market. But Keynesian income control policies cannot maintain balance as capitalism reaches an inflationary full employment phase. As we have seen, inflation is accompanied by a distorted upwriting of the price-wage fabric. An imbalance is thus created which causes gross unfairness and depressions.

The current power problem of capitalism has to do with the proper upwriting of the price-wage fabric. Power in modern capitalism has become greatly concentrated. *The effect of power concentration is to distort the price-wage fabric and cause imbalance, since those with power (1) do not act in the general interest, but in their own special interests, and (2) do not possess any theory, principles, or policies upon which the general interest can be rationally based.* The true model of modern corporate capitalism is one of power concentrates which promote imbalance. *There is no central directing force inherent in corporate capitalism* to provide planning, coordination, balance, and the promotion of the general interest.

As a result, if the general interest is promoted, this happy event comes about (1) by accident, or (2) because special interests and general interests happen to coincide, or (3) because the Federal Government intervenes to support the general interest in response to the pressure of public opinion. There are two possibilities therefore for the restoration of balance and support of the general interest through centralized control of the economy. Either (1) the major power groups which frequently make basic policy decisions must act in the general interest and assume a paternalistic role, or (2) the general interest must be implemented by the general public through the action of the Federal Government.

"THE POWER ÉLITE"

Something like a power élite or super power group exists which to a considerable extent controls our politico-economic society. It consists of large corporations, the very wealthy who are active in business, union leaders, top military men, the political leaders and the President and his top administrators. It is of vital importance as a pivotal factor in the solution of the current power problem and in the preservation of the democratic organization of American society. What is its true character? Certainly it is not as powerful or as unified as people like Mills suppose. It is less military than it was under Eisenhower, despite the fact that the American economy is geared to defense production, and defense expenditures play a great part in determining the size and stability of our gross national product. Perhaps one could regard it as sharing power with the general public at times, as being, on occasion, overruled by the general public, but for the most part making important policy decisions on an interim basis while the general public remains dormant. Public power versus élite power is intermittent. It appears at times of crisis or failure in the decisions of the power groups. Public power became dominant in the early days of the Roosevelt administration and became dormant as businessmen infiltrated the administration during the war years. Under Truman, public power flared up again. Under Eisenhower, however, there were eight years of dormancy with some reawakening in the elections of Kennedy and Johnson.

Since the power groups, through their control over economic life and over the federal administration, more often than not dominate American economic and political policy, it is essential to know their composition, goals, and capability of promoting the general interest. As to the "élite's" composition, the corporate chief executives predominate. It is easy to overemphasize the role of very wealthy men. It is apparent that although the Fords, Rockefellers, Hunts, and Cullens have great power, they are in the minority of the political power groups, and are not always active politically. The typical "ruler" of America is the chief executive of a large corporation who has come up through the ranks of the corporate bureaucracy through selection by his superiors.

What are the goals and characteristics of these men? The profit motive is not always paramount. Businessmen are interested in power and prestige, in production and efficiency. Large profits are sought, but steadiness and security of profits are often as important as the amounts. There has also developed a sense of social leadership, since large institutions with thousands of stockholders, workers, and consumers are involved. There is a tendency of chief executives to express sentiments of social obligation, whether they always live up to them or not. They are inclined to consider themselves not only as profit-makers and administrators, but as public trustees. In addition, they have a strong desire to preserve capitalism as they conceive of it, to support national defense and to thwart the expansion of communism. In determining both economic and political policy, however, they are pragmatic and interest-minded. They do not operate upon a body of principles or general philosophy of the public interest. When called upon for principles, they often revert to classical economics and the virtues of competition, for want of any other theories to turn to. The principles they express are likely to be unrelated to their actual policies, not because of hypocrisy, but because of the lack of new modern capitalistic principles.

This fact goes far toward explaining their apparent anxiety and lack of confidence. Leading businessmen in America have unusual power and prestige, and it is not confined to the business world. Although they hold an exalted position, they are often uneasy about it. They exhibit at times defensiveness, suspicion, and pessimism. They fear that the public is anti-business, and they are concerned about organized labor and the skepticism of intellectuals about business.[1] As Worthy says, "For all the undoubted power and prestige

1 *Cf.*, Worthy, J. C., *Big Business and Free Men*, pp. 3-5

of the businessman in contemporary society, he is frequently ill at ease." [1]

It has been asserted by Mills and others that the top corporate executives lack stable morality, and are ignorant and intellectually mediocre. If these characteristics are valid, there is much reason for concern. In a society which has become extremely complicated and scientific, and which requires subordination of special to general interests for its preservation and growth, major decisions should be made by men who are moral, well-educated, and intelligent. Today's men of power are probably more amoral than immoral, and they could be highly moral if the principles of capitalism were reconstructed. How can there be any stable corporate morality when the changing corporate capitalism has been neither wholly described nor adequately defended?

To sum it up, the groups exercising great power in our society consist largely of the chief corporate executives. Although these men are profit-motivated, they are also concerned with power, prestige, production, efficiency, security, the future of capitalism, and the dangers of communism. They have also a growing sense of social responsibility and social trusteeship. They are anxious about their social position and the approval of the general public. They are pragmatic and lack a working corporate philosophy. They are more amoral than immoral, more socially and organizationally-minded than cultured and intellectual.

THE RESPONSIBILITIES OF THE CORPORATE ÉLITE

But in the light of their outlined qualities, the crucial question is: are they capable of exercising a stewardship over the economy and the Government in the general interest and in terms of general principles of balance? This question can only be answered, if at all, in terms of the role that chief executives play within the emerging corporate society.

[1] *Ibid.*, p. 6

The character of the modern corporation and its property and functional relationships determine the character of the modern corporation executive and his capability of serving as a trustee for society as a whole. The changing character of the great corporation serves as the basis for the assumption by chief executives of a broad social role. If they cannot assume this role, government will have to assume it. If economic balance in our society is to be attained through the policies and actions of corporate power groups rather than through government control, those who direct our great corporations, and through them the core of our economic system, must assume a general rather than a special interest position. It is difficult for businessmen to contemplate such a broad role, or to accept the great responsibilities inherent in it, but no alternative exists apart from further growth of governmental economic responsibility.

Having accumulated and concentrated economic power, the large corporation has created an economic situation requiring a degree of centralization in economic planning. Either large corporations must cooperate to plan for the economic system as a whole, or they invite by their inaction further government intervention. If one of the fundamentals of capitalism is a minimum of statism, business must continue to prove, in this respect as in others, that the essentials of economic life can be more efficiently handled by private enterprise and that individual wants and freedom are better served by it than by further extension of government enterprise.

What then will convert the great corporation executive into a broader public servant? In other words, what will prevent him from saying, "the welfare of the United States is the welfare of the XYZ Corporation of which I am president"? Some leading executives today, of course, need little conversion, but their timidity or modesty concerning the assumption of such a broad social role may make them hesitate to assume it. Conviction in this regard which will lead to positive social action depends on understanding and acceptance of the great changes which have resulted from the evolution of the large corporation. There is need for a new body of ethics, morality, and principles related to our corporate power society. If these are developed and accepted, there is no reason why the great corporate executive should not frankly and without fear assume broad leadership.

In our present stage of transition between old and new thought, this will take time. If too much time elapses, however, social problems may become acute. Others will jump in where the "business angels" fear to tread. Or is it fear? It may be indifference, traditionalism, or obscurantism. Whatever the cause, greater understanding of the nature of the large corporation and its social significance is basic to removal of the inhibition.

THE SOCIAL NATURE OF THE LARGE CORPORATION [1]

In the second half of the nineteenth and the first half of the twentieth centuries the world was in a period of revolutionary change. Not only were there socialist, fascist, and communist revolutions; capitalism also underwent revolution in ways no less fundamental, although less obvious. The primary purpose of revolution in all these forms of economy was the reorganization of social, political, and economic institutions in such a way that mechanical and chemical technology could provide a much greater volume of goods and a higher standard of living. Socialist and communist revolutions sought this result through state ownership and control of the means of production. Fascism sought economic reorganization for both economic and military reasons through rigid totalitarian state control. The capitalist revolution

[1] The author is greatly indebted to Adolf Berle, Jr., for many of the views expressed in the following pages. Cf., Berle, A., Jr., *The Twentieth Century Capitalist Revolution* and *Power without Property*.

achieved greater production and higher living standards through the organizing, controlling, and planning influences of the large corporation. A high degree of collectivism was thus achieved, but the resulting system was nonstatist and preserved some of the main elements of private property. It is unrealistic to consider these hundred years as revolutionary in only the socialist and communist nations. As Berle has said, the corporations "have been essentially revolutionary instruments in twentieth century capitalism . . . they have been one cause, if not the major cause, of its evolution to a state undreamed of in earlier economic theory." [1]

A by-product of corporate collectivism is the concentration of power. Only through a high degree of concentration could large-scale efficient and planned production be achieved. On this integrated, coordinated, planned, mass enterprise our great production depends. The corporations provide the collectivism needed for large output, and the results were greater than have been achieved through socialist and communist statist collectivism. If concentrated power is an evil, it is an essential evil, a price which must be paid for the growth of production to high levels. It was necessary for the twentieth century "explosion" of technology.

The resulting concentration of power is both internal and external. Internally, power is exercised by corporate management over individuals. They are hired and fired, given certain working conditions, and promoted or denied opportunity. Externally, the corporation determines when, where and how things are produced, from whom it will buy, the nature of the product it will sell to consumers, the prices of the goods, the dividends given to stockholders, and the location of businesses and the communities around them. As we have seen, these powers ramify into other industries and businesses, into social life, into government, and into philanthropy and research.

1 Berle, A., Jr., *The Twentieth Century Capitalist Revolution*, p. 17

It is often said that we live in a "mixed economy." For example, our economy is neither purely competitive nor purely monopolistic. In addition, our economy is neither wholly private nor public. Government enterprise functions alongside private enterprise. There are gradations here. A public utility is neither entirely private nor entirely public, and some have called public utilities quasi- or semi-public institutions. Even the large private corporations are called "public" corporations. They are "public" because of the degree of control and influence they exercise and the large number of workers and stockholders they have. They are no longer private in the sense that small machine shops or beauty parlors are. They have created a mixed economy by creating both mixed institutions and mixed economic practices.

The large corporation, in addition to becoming a public institution, has evolved a form of business which is both economic and political. The politico-economic aspects of the large public corporation can be briefly summarized as follows:

(1) The corporation is a creature of the state and its purposes must be approved by the state. It cannot exceed them without becoming *ultra vires.*

(2) The large corporation is regulated by government in a great number of ways as regards its production, employment, sales practices, price practices, and security issues.

(3) Government is the greatest business partner in any large corporation because it takes a very large part of its peacetime profits and, in wartime, even ninety-five percent of its excess profits.

(4) Many corporations depend on government purchases for a large part of their business and are intimately bound up with government procurement and research.

(5) Many large corporations depend on government as an important source of capital and lease a large part of their productive facilities from the government.

(6) Large corporations are essentially nonstatist political institutions in that they have public responsibilities and "constituencies."

THE CORPORATION AS A FORM OF GOVERNMENT

The last of these political features is the most important. The original governmental design of the corporation was democratic. All power was vested in the stockholders acting as a group at the annual stockholders' meeting or at special meetings. In the beginning, stockholders voted as individuals, having one vote regardless of the number of corporate shares they owned. Very early, however, voting changed to a shares basis. The stockholders presumably determined business policy, and they elected a higher policy body, the board of directors, to act for them in the interim between stockholders' meetings. The directors in their turn elected the president, who served as the executive of the corporation along with his appointed staff. Thus, the stockholders were a *constituency* to which the directors and executive were responsible.

But the nature of this constituency has changed as a result of the growth in the size of the corporation. It consists of not only the stockholders, but the employees, the concerns selling goods to the corporation, the consumers of corporate products, the local community, and the state and Federal governments. This broader constituency must be recognized. Corporations have become so large and have such broad effects on people's lives as to constitute public institutions responsible in many ways for public welfare. It will not be recognized, however, if corporations are regarded merely as profit-making institutions responsible only to the stockholders. But how can AT & T, General Motors, United States Steel and other leviathans still be considered solely as private profit-making businesses responsible only to their stockholders?

The governmental character of the large corporation is

well illustrated by a consideration of the rights and opportunities of individuals and businesses that it affects. Berle
has given examples from two fields: the right to work and the
right of dealers to sell corporate property. Discharge by a
large corporation may make thousands not only jobless, but
even permanently jobless. Under present security arrangements, large corporations engaged in defense production,
like General Electric, may be called upon to discharge employees for "security reasons." Employees thus discharged
may become permanently jobless, or at least unable to obtain
their customary form of employment, unless they can appeal
their discharges successfully. In the absence of protective laws
requiring appeals and the showing of cause, such employees
are deprived of their jobs and the right to work at the discretion of the corporation. When businesses were small, and
when they could not stigmatize workers as unemployable, a
worker discharged by one concern could eventually obtain
employment from another. *Businesses did not grant or deny
the right to work.* They were not governments. In denying
the right to work, a large corporation has assumed a government function.

The discharge of employees for security reasons is an extreme example of a large corporation's determination of the
right to work. In only a somewhat lesser degree, the decision
of corporations to cut production also denies the right to
work. Thousands have been thrown out of work since 1956
in the automobile industry, and few of these have any genuine
opportunity to obtain employment in work for which they
are fitted. Large hard cores of unemployment are appearing
in many fields, due to automation. The solution would
seem to be retraining for other types of work. But the possibilities of industrial retraining or reallocation can be exaggerated. When large corporations (a) decide to cut back
production, (b) to reduce the retirement age, (c) to automate,
or (d) to move to another community, they cause serious un-

employment which, in effect, denies the right to work to many thousands, if not permanently, at least for a long period. These effects did not result from business decisions when corporations were small and workers could be employed by others. Now whole communities dependent on one or two large corporations may be wrecked by corporate decisions. *Corporations in these instances are not so much businesses as governments and are assuming govermental rather than economic powers.*

A corollary to the governmental character of large corporations is the fact that corporate executives, except perhaps at the very top, are becoming less and less like traditional profit-seeking business men and more like government civil servants. Although some of the characteristics of civil servants are lacking, other essential traits and concerns are present. Among these are concern over job security, concern over organization status, interest in a career of rising through the ranks of the organization, organization-mindedness, pension-consciousness, desire for power and desire for prestige. But corporation executives may frequently get to the very top through association rather than through merit, and there are, in the higher ranks, no standard job descriptions or regularized standards for promotion. However, this is also true of government. Positions at the very top may be filled on a political rather than a civil service basis.

THE CORPORATION AND PROPERTY

The concentrated, powerful, revolutionary, collectivist, and political character of the large modern corporation can be understood by examining the changing relationship of owners to property, caused by its evolution. Private property has been transformed through the corporation into a form of semipublic property. Theoretically, private property consists of the unlimited possession of things, including the rights of (1) ownership, (2) use, (3) control, (4) receipt of income, and

(5) transference. Thus, without limit, an individual had a right to own, use, control, receive income from, and dispose of his property which was largely, in times past, in tangible physical form. Perhaps farm land best illustrated this early private possessory form of property. The corporation, however, is an aggregate of property ownership of an intangible nature. An individual does not own specific physical parcels of corporate property, but has an equity or beneficial interest in a part of the aggregate. Corporate property is not a relationship of people to a thing or *res,* but a complex of relationships of individuals to each other.[1]

Corporations "split the atom" of property. Ownership, although of shares rather than of things, remained technically with the stockholder. But use and control were transferred to the management and their employees. Much of the income went to these two groups also. The stockholder, moreover, retained rights of disposal and transference, but again of shares, not of things. The owner, or stockholder, was thus separated from use and control of property in the so-called separation of ownership and management. Stockholders retained three rights: (1) to receive dividends, (2) to share in dissolution, and (3) to vote.

Loss of the use of property did not by itself mean loss of control of a general sort through the determination of business policy so long as the stockholder retained the right to vote. Looked at from a legal viewpoint, the stockholder had merely delegated *detailed* control to the management, but could still determine the broad outlines and direction of control through stockholders' meetings and the election of directors. But with the dispersion of ownership among thousands of stockholders, this view became unrealistic. Stockholders seldom were confronted with the real issues, and when they were, the management controlled the votes through the proxy system. For the most part, actual control as well as use

[1] *Cf.* Berle, Adolf, Jr., *Power without Property,* Ch. 2

was lost by the majority of stockholders to a small minority of rich stockholders, to the management, or to a combination of both. Real corporate power was thus concentrated in the hands of a few people who often held an infinitesimal percentage of the total voting stock. Although the dispersion of ownership was enough to effect concentration of power in most corporations, the proxy device, class voting, nonvoting common stock, nonvoting preferred stock, multiple voting, and the pyramiding of holding companies exaggerated these tendencies. In more recent years the payment of money by millions of individuals for insurance premiums and mutual and pension funds still further separates the real owners of corporate property from control and management. In insurance and mutual and pension funds the owers have even lost the right to vote, ceremonial though that may be for the stockholder in most large corporations.

The changing property relationships in the corporation gave rise to a politico-economic control structure in big business. The businesses involved were not controlled by the owners. Owners assumed a passive-receptive role. The corporate organization and management, on the other hand, assumed the functions of creation. They were responsible for productive results. They became organized in a managerial pyramid with workers at the broad base and with several levels of executives above them. As a large complicated organization, they assumed the aspects of a government bureaucracy. Typical governmental civil service problems arose: job description, job rating, seniority rights, tenure rights, pension rights, promotion, internal communication, internal harmony, and coordination. Corporation executives were not capitalists, since they did not own the capital they controlled. Since they did not own the capital, they were less concerned with high profits and more concerned with steady profits, status, prestige, power, high salaries, bonuses, and large pensions. They were men of power and prestige who managed other people's money. As such, they began to appear more as trustees than as capitalists and unlike the top businessmen of the last century, they seldom became extremely wealthy. They did not have to be. When Walter F. Gifford retired from AT & T, his pension of over $80,000 a year was the equivalent of about $1,500,000 of wealth.

MANAGERIAL ENTERPRISE

Thus, with the dominance of the large corporation, a new governmental managerial economy has arisen which is accompanied by changing attitudes toward the principles of individual enterprise and property. It requires, as we have said before, a new set of principles, ethics, and morality. A broader term would be a new corporate ideology from which principles and morals could be derived.

To a large extent modern power rests on ideology, although we seem to resist any philosophical approaches in the United States except traditionalism and pragmatism. We shy away from philosophy and social theory, claiming that they are impractical. They may have been of limited use in a competitive, individualistic society, and especially one which was not power-structured. Once power, planning, and great organization appear, ideology becomes a necessary concomitant. Berle points out that there are two types of power, brute *de facto* domination through physical force, and power which commands and is based on allegiance, loyalty, and cooperation. These cannot be elicited unless there is popular understanding of the reasons for and benefits from the concentration of power. Without this understanding and popular acquiescence, power is unstable. These considerations have led Berle to state bluntly that "the effectiveness and continuity of power itself thus rests on an ideological structure." [1]

[1] Berle, *op. cit.*, p. 80

CONCLUSIONS

In a broad way we have now described the main features of our politico-economic society within the structure of which our current power problem must be solved. We have provided the bare outlines, at least, of a politico-economic model necessary for its solution. The model reveals the dominance of the large corporation. The executives who control these great public corporate politico-economic bodies are not only individually the holders of great power, but the leaders of a power group which—instead of Congress or the general public—intermittently controls the nation. In view of these facts, the large corporations and the corporate élite must supply the planning and coordination of economic life needed for the balance which their managerial enterprise system requires. They have displaced the old balancing elements inherent in the free market and free enterprise. They cannot rely on the market price system to balance the economy. They must lead a new corporate planned society. If they do not provide the necessary leadership for economic balance and growth, government will step into the leadership vacuum. But to lead, they must have morals, principles, and theories of economic balance valid for the new corporate society, and they must have the courage to lead. All these are requirements which are sadly lacking. We lack a new corporate ideology and morality and a theory of economic balance which fits the new corporate society.

XI

Economic Solutions for the Power Problem

———

No one person has all the facts or wisdom needed to propose an overall solution of the American power problem. Furthermore, no solutions are worthy of much consideration which are tangential or highly specialized. Two conclusions should be obvious from the study of the problem. First, it cannot be dealt with in a timid or peripheral manner with overconcern for what is or is not politically feasible. Second, the problem is very complex and has a long historical background. Suggestions for solution must be as comprehensive and complex as the problem itself.

The efficiency and glamour of the great American corporations and the growing social responsibility of the men who lead them make it very tempting to accept the thesis that the corporate executives can and will plan for the general interest. To some extent, they are already doing it. But because it cannot be assumed that all the conditions necessary for corporate leadership are now or will be present in the near future, we cannot expect corporate executives to solve the power problem. They are not yet ready to accept broad impartial social leadership, to be guided always by the public consensus, to accept legal review of their power, to endorse further centralization in economic planning, and to develop a broad social philosophy of corporate capitalism which will guide them. No doubt corporate leaders will become progressively more social-minded in working out their broad economic plans. But it is our conclusion that the main solution of the power problem must come from the Federal Government.

At the heart of any solution is the general interest. Concentrated power has disturbed the balance in economic, political, and social life because it has biased the nation's social processes in the direction of special interests. Only through a return to some concept of the general interest can our power problems be solved. To make this suggestion is neither fascist nor communist. It can be regarded as traditional. The most cursory examination of the writings of our early statesmen in such documents as the *Federalist Papers* reveals that they considered the public interest to be paramount. They seem to have understood the dangers of pressure groups and the concentration of power as well as, if not better than, we do today. Their conception of government was not a struggle between power groups in which one triumphed over the others. They wanted a government of impartial and thoughtful men who would place the welfare of the whole above that of any individual or group. Many of our presidents have accepted this point of view. The most noteworthy was Wilson, but in recent years Truman, Kennedy, and Johnson have returned to the concept of the general interest.

THE OLDER SOLUTIONS

With the conclusion that the Federal Government should provide the main power solutions based upon the concept of the general interest, we can turn to specific proposals. First, some of the older approaches to the power problem still have value and should be pursued to the extent of their usefulness.

(1) One of these is *the application of the Sherman Antitrust Act.* A prominent member of the Federal Trade Commission has contended that there are many instances where

bigness beyond a point is productive not only of monopolistic practices, but of economic inefficiency. There is no reason why the antitrust law cannot still be enforced to the extent of preventing mergers which lessen competition. It can also be used to prevent extreme price-fixing practices, as in the case of the General Electric Company. Vigorous Attorney Generals have found ample scope for the enforcement of the Sherman and Federal Trade Commission acts. The concentration of power, having become great, need not become greater. What has been done cannot always be undone, but what is on the verge of being done can be prevented.[1]

(2) Another older solution is the *regulation of competition*. It has become conventional to minimize the work of the Federal Trade Commission. Out of many cases of unfair competition which are investigated, only a few are the subject of cease and desist orders. But standards of fair competition which tend to protect the consumer and the small business man have been established in many fields as a result of the work of the Commission. Conformity has been extensive. The value of the Commission's work can hardly be measured by the number of violations it has punished. In all its years of operation, also, it has been hampered by an inadequate budget and limited personnel. Despite these handicaps, it has done valuable work which should be continued and strengthened. Both the antitrust laws and the Commission have long been disregarded as the main means of solving our power problems, but they remain as adjuncts to the solution which are too important to be ignored or allowed to languish.

(3) Another solution of far greater importance is *fiscal*

---

[1] *Cf.* Wilcox, Clair, *Public Policies Toward Business*, p. 876. Professor Wilcox, an outstanding student of the relation of government to business, has concluded that "the antitrust laws have been influential in preserving market freedom. The courts have been consistent in their condemnation of restrictive agreements and monopolistic practices. They have been effective in striking down barriers to competitive enterprise. They have displayed discretion and common sense in dealing with combination and monopoly."

policy—the tax and expenditure system of the Federal Government coupled at times with cooperative action by state governments. In general, the Federal Government should use deficits and surpluses consciously to reduce depression and curb inflation. The surpluses and deficits are the primary means by which the amount of the flow of money income can be controlled. Rigorous adherence to high taxes and budget surpluses can limit inflation. The reverse policy has been the only effective means of making the economy recover from a depression.

But fiscal policy must be coordinated with other controls. The nature of it should be planned in relationship to the recommendations of the President's Council of Economic Advisers. It must always be realized that its control power in inflation is seriously limited by the upwriting of the price-wage fabric by power groups. Some form of price control must run parallel to fiscal policy if inflation is to be prevented. Above all, it should not be made a tool of interest groups. When large corporations want to raise prices, or unions, wages, they should not be assisted in these objectives by the Federal Government. More money income should not be created by means of deficits so that consumers may buy at the higher prices. The deficits for defense spending after World War II were a very convenient inflation tool for both big business and big labor. Without them, the wage-price spiral would have been impossible. But fiscal policy should be the servant of the general, not the special, interests of the nation.

Fiscal policy can be used for specific controls as well as a general control device. A description of the specialized use of taxes and public expenditures for economic control would require many pages. Only a few generalizations and examples can be given here. It is well known that one factor in the development of the depression and inflationary phases of the economy is the rate of saving. The location of saving is in the higher brackets of income. By making taxes more progressive so that they fall more heavily on the higher income groups, saving can be reduced and spending increased to promote recovery from a depression. Contrariwise, saving can be increased by making taxes more regressive, in other words, by shifting the burden to the lower income groups. In this way, spending is cut down and inflation curbed. The tax system should be consciously adjusted to suit depression and inflation. But since tax laws cannot be changed without lengthy legislative processes which sometimes unduly delay or make ineffective the controls proposed, the President should be given discretionary powers to change the tax structure quickly to adjust it to the changing economic scene.

Taxes may be used even more specifically to deal with unfairness and inequality resulting from power group influences. Corporate executives and persons of wealth today are greatly favored by numerous tax loopholes, or, as some prefer to call them, tax "shelters." Part of the reward for power is tax privilege. An administration in Washington that concerns itself with the welfare of the average man should work vigorously to reduce or eliminate the many tax loopholes available to the wealthy. Many other changes can be made in the federal tax system which would offset some of the ill effects of economic power concentration. For example, taxes could be reduced on small businesses and corporations with net income of less than a million dollars a year. Peacetime excess profits taxation is another possibility, but one which would arouse great business opposition. In general, business taxation should promote fairness as between small and large businesses and provide incentives for the productive investment of capital. The latter is especially important in periods of depression or lagging economic growth. The tax system should be made as flexible as possible to fit changes in economic activity. Tariffs also, another form of taxation, should be adjusted to the needs for economic growth and not be used to create monopolistic privileges for special groups of workers and business men.

In addition to taxes, there are tremendous possibilities for the achievement of economic balance through the planned use of public expenditures. In depressions, expenditures for relief and the extension of unemployment compensation benefits are not only devices to relieve distress, but serve to restore the spending and purchasing power needed to bring recovery. Galbraith has emphasized the need for "redress" in the social investment balance. By this is meant that a greater proportion of capital should be invested in schools, hospitals, housing, and for other social purposes. Since private enterprise cannot be expected to restore this balance, the task is the responsibility of the Federal Government. For many years, there has been a critical need for greater progress in the field of low cost housing. Senator Robert Wagner was especially concerned with this problem and through his efforts the Federal Government began a program of aid during the depression period. In 1946, after the war, liberals placed public housing high on their agenda for social progress, but little has been accomplished despite the great wealth of our nation. Many poorer countries are far ahead of us in solving slum problems. The situation is similarly critical in the fields of hospitals, recreational facilities, and aid to education. The colleges of the country face a serious need to provide facilities for housing and teaching the greatly growing student population. Various forms of research need aid also. "Social" expenditures of the Federal Government should be increased at least a hundred percent in the next ten years. But here again, opposition is likely to be extreme, especially in such areas as "socialized" medicine or the extension of the benefits and coverage of our social security system.

Fiscal policy, whether we regard it from the standpoint of

taxes or of expenditures, is the greatest instrument of indirect control for economic planning in the United States. The traditional view of taxes is that they are merely revenue devices. The traditional view of public expenditure is to regard it as a necessary evil which should be held to a minimum. Growing public expenditure is viewed with alarm as either inflationary or as a form of "creeping socialism." We are unable to admit that expenditures by government may be an important means of avoiding socialism. The willingness to allow the persistence of bad housing, inadequate education, shortage of hospital beds, inadequate community services, insufficient recreation facilities, inadequate care of the aged, inadequate medical care, and insufficient research facilities in an affluent society could well lead to socialism in the long run. An immediate danger arises from our failure to use public expenditures as a device to ease transitional distress caused by the rapid growth of automation. We cannot allow millions of people to become unemployed for this reason without aid. We face the same type of problem that developed in the twenties and was then called technological unemployment. Willingness in those days to contemplate a growing hard core of persistent unemployment without aid was a factor in causing the catastrophe of 1929.

Thus our view of fiscal policy must be modernized and freed from obstruction by the false fear of socialism. To modernize it is first to recognize its vital importance as a means of economic and social balance and to give up the notion that taxes should be only revenue devices. To modernize it means also that it should be used as a vast planning device that offsets the decline of the free market as an efficient allocator of resources. As a planning device, it should be integrated with economic planning in government and business in general. Ideally, fiscal policy should no longer be determined by the whims or pressures of interest groups. It should be related to an overall or master plan for the growth of American economic and social life. *It should be in the general interest.*

(4) Another older solution is *countervailing power* and various forms of economic pluralism. Here again, the limitations of these balancing devices as revealed by their past performance should not result in complete cynicism. Granted that not everything can be expected of them, can we conclude that *nothing* can be expected of them? One reason for the weakness of countervailing power is that unions do not persist in using it through adhering to true collective bargaining. A simple example may illustrate the point. A business may have a certain amount of anticipated gross receipts and a given level of costs. Wages are an important cost element. The workers of the firm request higher wages and a period of bargaining begins. The dispute is, or should be, over the distribution of the firm's surplus earnings. Will management take less profit in order to allow the workers higher wages? Can the union force it to do this? But often collective bargaining which involves true countervailing power turns into labor-management collusion. How this happens can be made clearer through a *reductio ad absurdum*. Let us assume that labor and management agree that management cannot afford to take less profit. But the workers want higher wages, so the president of the company proposes to the union leader that they go together and rob a bank. With other people's money thus obtained, they will be able to pay the higher wages. This is really what happens when unions take higher wages knowing that the result will be higher prices. The employer and the union rob not one bank but the many banks in which their customers are depositors.

Of course, it may be asked, what can unions really do about this sort of situation? Is it not reasonable, in an inflationary period, for unions to demand higher wages? After the higher wages are granted, are unions responsible if corporations raise prices to get the money from the general public?

The answer, of course, is no. But we should expect organized labor to take a firm stand against higher prices and not collaborate with corporations to get higher wages through higher prices. They should support the efforts of the Federal Government to curb inflation. In refusing to accept rising labor productivity as the only valid basis for higher wages, or in insisting that the increase of productivity be defined solely as the result of labor effort, they are indirectly justifying higher prices as the means of higher wages, in other words, the robbery of the general public. Collective bargaining is not the gouging of outsiders. It is bargaining over the distribution of the income *internal* to a business or industry. When either labor or management views it as a means of getting income from the general public (and it has not been unknown for management to raise prices by more than the cost of the wage increase) it is not collective bargaining. *It is a monopolistic conspiracy to raise prices which in another form would be regarded as a flagrant violation of antitrust law.*

In spite of this, the record of unionism is not all black. True collective bargaining has existed for many years. It has performed a service not only in protecting the rights of labor, but in promoting balance in the economy by insuring that wages rise with labor productivity and that spendable incomes increase as more income is earned. It is therefore useful in solving the power problem resulting from economic unbalance. But it is much more effective for this purpose during depressions than in a period of inflation. The creation of excess purchasing power by the government provides a serious temptation to use collective bargaining as a price-raising or unbalancing device. Perhaps it can be said that the real responsibility for wrongdoing lies with the government. Through fiscal measures it should prevent excess purchasing power. Especially it should not, as in the Eisenhower Administration, indulge in tacit collaboration with big labor and big business by failing to take any vigorous steps against the price-raising process and by further unbalancing the budget so that a price-wage spiral is made possible.[1]

There are other forms of economic pluralism besides collective bargaining, such as oligopsony, or the countervailing power exercised by large buyers like the chain stores. There is also an element of countervailing power in oligopoly. Occasionally the three or four corporate giants in an industry will indulge in price competition. Whether this happens or not, its possibility may serve to restrain the large corporations from monopolistic price policies. In a few segments of the economy, cooperatives also play a part in providing a form of balance through group competition. These pluralistic tendencies, although of very limited significance, should be encouraged for whatever value they have.

(5) Another and much neglected older approach is *consumer representation and protection*. Beginning with the Pure Food and Drug Act and the establishment of the Federal Bureau of Standards, there has been a slowly increasing representation of the consumer interest. Numerous state laws have been passed relating to sales practices, the quality of products, fairness in selling and advertising, and even in some cases, pricing. Fifteen states have pure food and drug acts. But consumer legislation is largely designed to restrict injurious products, provide information and prevent the consumer from being cheated. Only in a minor degree is it concerned with prices and inflation. Consumer representation in the price determination process began during the NRA, but was abandoned on the Federal level when the NRA was declared unconstitutional.

As a balancing force, the consumer interest would be great if it could be organized. But this seems a hopeless task. Americans persist in regarding themselves only as producers. Al-

---

1 President Eisenhower's pleas against price raising did not constitute a vigorous attack on inflation. His strictures on the need for profit abstinence fell on deaf ears.

most any kind of occupation can be organized in some way, but we are not consumer-minded enough to organize for the protection of our interests as consumers except in cases of fraud and malpractice. Theoretically one might conceive of broad national anti-inflation societies. They have not appeared, but with shorter hours, earlier retirement, and greater preoccupation of men with household problems, the broader organization of consumers may be possible. If national consumer organizations could become strong, they could be represented in governmental regulative bodies and the cabinets of governors and of the President. Presumably, production is primarily for consumption and the consumer interest is more nearly the general interest than any form of specific producer interest such as that of management, farmers, labor, or the civil service.

(6) As another minor solution, the outright *promotion of competition* has some merit. Competition may be promoted through strengthening small business or through competitive government enterprise. Both have been tried with some success. The promotion of competition is the positive counterpart of the antitrust laws and the restraint of monopoly. The chief limitation on small and new competitive business is lack of capital. Small businesses, if they can survive long enough to prove their potential earning power, can usually borrow some working capital from banks. But investment banking is not set up in this country to assist small businesses to expand through the sale of stocks. They can obtain equity capital only from the reinvestment of earnings or the addition of partners. The heavy burden of the corporation income tax on small businesses makes expansion from earnings difficult. Our tax system is designed to promote large business. Small business is handicapped in many other ways. It cannot usually get government contracts and it has little or no money for research, for management consultants, and for advice in regard to its markets.

From time to time, the Federal Government has made efforts to aid small business. The Reconstruction Finance Corporation granted direct loans and insured loans made by banks. The Smaller War Plants Corporation and the Small Defense Plants Administration during World War II and the Korean War assisted small businesses to obtain government contracts. The Federal Government established a Small Business Administration to assist in various ways. But the large loans to small businesses disappeared when the RFC was abolished and no similar or comparable government program to finance small business replaced it. Some private financial organizations remain which are interested in making loans of long-term capital, but the need for small business capital is greater and the sources of it fewer than ever before. The promotion of small business and the competition that accompanies it would require the establishment of a large new federal lending agency.

Competition can also be promoted by the establishment of government enterprises in fields which are not fully meeting consumer needs. The outstanding example in this country is the Tennessee Valley Authority which supplied electricity and lowered prices in an area where private utilities had failed to provide for rural electrification. Government promoted competition in aluminum by first constructing aluminum plants during World War II and then by leasing and selling the plants to companies that would compete with the Aluminum Company of America, which had virtual monopoly status. President Truman threatened to construct government steel plants unless the steel industry expanded after World War II to meet the shortage of steel. But government competition has been tried more extensively in other countries. It has been used in many fields, including railroads. Its potential has never been sufficiently explored in the United States and there are many ways in which it might result in beneficial balancing effects. Opposition to it has been based on rather vague fears of socialism and even vaguer arguments as to the inefficiency of government enterprise.

THE MAJOR ROLE OF CAPITALIST GOVERNMENT PLANNING

The six older solutions are of some value and should be used to the extent of their effectiveness. But new approaches to the power problem are needed. The concentration of power in huge politico-economic groups has caused unbalance and an urgent need for greater centralization of planning and control. *This centralization through the forthright action of the Federal Government in the general interest is the main solution of the present-day power problem.* The planning contemplated is not socialism. It is a capitalist derivative of the development of concentrated corporate capitalism and its logical consequence.

Because the term planning has been used in a variety of ways, we need to define the sense in which it is used here. Inherent in planning in general is forecasting and conscious direction of the future. This can be done by economic control which is total or partial, centralized or decentralized, informational or regulatory. One may conceive of communist planning, socialist planning, or capitalist planning. *The planning we advocate is capitalist planning.* As such, it is not highly centralized. It is to a large extent partial, and it emphasizes information, guidance, and leadership rather than regulation. It will be contended that this is not planning at all; that planning cannot be capitalist, decentralized, and nonregulatory. But criticism along this line involves definitional objections rather than the denial of a potential form of capitalist planning. In fact, there has been a trend toward capitalist planning in the United States since the nineteen thirties. What is here proposed merely extends this trend.

The proposal of capitalist planning by government is derived from our conclusions that the corporate hierarchy is not ready to plan for the whole economy, that, according to our social hypothesis, the time has come, due to the extreme concentration of power, for greater centralization in planning to establish and maintain balance and growth, and that balance requires planning in the general interest of which the Federal Government is (as of now) the only capable and willing instrumentality. In order to make clear the nature of the planning proposed, we can outline it in terms of (1) the scope of things planned, (2) the degree of centralization, (3) the methods of planning, (4) the agencies used in planning and their responsibilities, (5) the economic and social theory behind the planning, (6) the planning goals, and (7) the controls and the degree of compulsion needed for the implementation of the planning.

(1) *Scope.* The Federal Government has engaged in a variety of planning operations for a number of years. To mention some of these fields, there is trade planning through the tariffs, planning of money and credit policy through the Treasury and the Federal Reserve System, planning of income flow through taxation and expenditure policies, planning of national defense, planning of roads, and planning of farm surplus control. What is proposed here is much more general, however. Put simply, *it is the planning of the income flow and the level of prices, wages, and output. Also proposed is a forecast of the needs and resources of the American economy, kept currently revised, and with a constant reformulation of American economic and social goals.* If planning of this scope were highly centralized and accompanied by extensive regulation, we would be dangerously near totalitarianism. But informational rather than extensive regulatory planning is the only form of planning consistent with capitalism.

(2) *The Degree of Centralization.* Where planning is highly centralized, as in the case of Soviet Russia, detailed information on output, wages, prices, and resources flows upward from the thousands of production units to the State

Planning Commission. This information is received and analyzed by the large statistical, economic, and engineering staff of the Commission. When a new plan is to be formulated, the Communist Party establishes the goals and transmits these to the Commission which then draws up a tentative plan to meet them. The plan is broken down into parts on a geographical and functional basis. The parts are then examined and discussed by regional and functional bodies. Revisions may be made on the basis of these discussions, but the discussions are mainly for the purpose of arousing interest and enthusiasm in the industry and regional planning committees. The parts are then returned with comments to the State Planning Commission which makes the final revisions. The revised plan is submitted to the Supreme Soviet for adoption. Once adopted, it is again divided and subdivided into parts until each factory, plant, trust, or collective farm has its plan, quota, prices, wages, and marketing instructions. These plans become directives for the operation of units during the life of the plan or until the plan is revised. Thus Soviet planning has been highly centralized and regulatory. Plans for every phase of Russian life are made and enforced by central governmental bodies. Little change results from suggestions by regional or functional bodies.

Capitalist planning must be decentralized. Suggestions for national goals, output levels, rates of growth, and price and wage levels must come from regional and functional groups to the Federal Government and merely be correlated on a democratic basis by the Federal planning agencies. The bodies suggesting plans would consist of corporations, unions, governments, and various professional, research, political, and party organizations. These suggestions would be incorporated into a national plan which would serve as a guiding or goal-setting device rather than as a detailed body of directives controlling every aspect of business and broken down into directives for the smallest productive units. But the decentralized character of capitalist planning is really an aspect of the methods of planning involved.

(3) *The Methods of Planning.* To plan in a free society is to set goals, guide lines, and limits to economic activity which can be modified and within which there remains much freedom of action. Planning is a democratic process in that it comes from the miscellaneous social and economic groupings, a bottom-to-top movement, and is subject to the approval of the general public. It is essentially informational, and, for purposes of leadership and only to a restricted extent, regulatory. It is partial rather than total, since, as we have pointed out not all aspects of social and economic life are planned, and the actual direction of economic processes remain decentralized in the hands of thousands of businessmen and farmers.

(4) *The Planning Agencies.* The planning agencies in capitalist planning would be both public and private. The private agencies might consist of a national planning committee in each industry. Their work could be supplemented by a labor planning committee and, if possible, a planning committee representing consumers. National organizations of business like the National Association of Manufacturers and the Committee for Economic Development might combine to form a central business planning committee. On the government level, state and local planning bodies would be required to make recommendations. On the Federal level, the main planning bodies would be the Bureau of the Budget; the Joint Committee of Congress on the President's Economic Report; the Treasury; the Board of Governors of the Federal Reserve System; the Tariff Commission; the Departments of Agriculture, Commerce, and Labor; the Maritime Commission; the Civil Aeronautics Board; the Federal Communications Commission; the Bureau of Roads; the Bureau of Mines; the National Atomic Energy Commission; the Joint

Military Chiefs of Staff; and the procurement divisions of the defense departments. All these agencies could report for the purpose of planning to the President's Council of Economic Advisers. A *National Planning Board* could be established representing Government through the President's Council of Economic Advisers, business through the NAM and CED, labor through the labor planning committee and one representative each for farmers and consumers. The NPB would determine planning policy and the President's Council of Economic Advisers would be given technical and clerical assistance enabling it to formulate a master plan based on this policy. The master plan might then be ratified by Congress. What is intended here is democratic planning by the leaders of all aspects of the American economy. The master plan would finally have democratic approval through Congressional action. But Congress could not do the planning. It should confine itself to acceptance or rejection of the plan with modifications.

(5) *Economic and Social Theory.* But such a large planning operation involving the participation of many individuals and groups would become a vast incoherent national busy-work project unless it was based on the acceptance of some form of economic theory. The facts gathered could be used in inconsistent ways if differently interpreted. No plan would have any value unless it was based consistently on one sound body of economic theory. But what is the needed body of theory? Classical economics, of course, must be largely discarded, and the Keynesian general theory can only be accepted with modifications based on latest thought. More than Keynesian or neo-Keynesian theory, however, would be needed. A theory of economic balance based on institutional analysis of price practices and related to the upwriting of the price-wage fabric would have to supplement Keynesianism.

The development of such a supplement is possible. But it

is a subject too extensive and complicated to be discussed here. A few examples may be given, however, of the types of analysis needed. For example, one of the basic factors in unbalance is the tendency of wages to rise too little in some economic situations and too much in others. The basic measure of the proper rise of wages is labor productivity. A theory related to labor productivity, which might be called the *Theory of Balanced Wage Rise* is needed as a guide. On the lower side of the balance is a depression tendency; above it, an inflationary tendency. The new and detailed theoretical instruments would have to measure and promote balance, *since the main purpose of planning is balance.* Another balancing concept might be called *Income Parity.* In fact, the term parity is applicable to all the measures we are proposing here. Thus balanced wage rise could be called *Wage Parity* and we already have in use a dubious concept which might be valid if revised—*Farm Price Parity.* All forms of income can have their parities such as *Profit Parity, Rent Parity, Salary Parity,* etc.

Over all is an *Income Parity.* By this we mean that on the average prices cannot rise faster than the spendable money income without causing first inflation and then depression. One can assume that as of a given year of full or near full employment spendable incomes and prices are at respective levels which constitute a norm. We have thus the formula $\frac{PI}{DI}$ equals 100, in which PI is the index of consumer prices in the parity or full employment year and DI the disposable money income in that year. If in the parity year, chosen because of the existence of full employment and defined as a year of minimum unemployment, the amount of DI or disposable income is $600 billion and the consumer price index is 150, then the parity dividend which equals the income parity index of 100 is $4 billion. We can derive from this a formula for determining the income parity index in preceding and subsequent years. It would be PD, or parity dividend, is to 100 as PD^1 or PD^2 or PD^{-1} and PD^{-2} are to X as we go forward or backward from the chosen parity year. Thus if in year "one," DI^1 is $600 billion and PI^1 is 200, PD^1 is $3 billion. Applying our formula for the computation of the parity index in year "one," we find it has fallen to 75. A critical problem of purchasing power has developed because of the upwriting of the price-wage fabric. A depression of serious proportions is being germinated. Either prices will have to come down or DI will have to rise with prices held stable. If, however, in year "one" DI had risen to $800 billion as prices rose to 200, the parity income index would have remained stable at 100, or the full employment level.

If the income parity analysis has validity, an index of income parity could be an important theoretical planning device. Prices could be planned in terms of the disposable income or vice versa. Presumably both should rise at the same rate or an inflation depression will be generated. If disposable income rises while prices remain constant, the situation may also promote depression, even though the index of income parity rises, because saving may be greatly increased and exceed the amount of investment which business men are willing to make at full employment. At this point another parity measure may be needed which could be called the *Investment Parity* or the volume of saving over the volume of investment. These must equal. If I, or investment, over S, or saving, is less than one, there will either be depression or a stoppage in the rate of growth. If it is greater than one, there will be inflation. The rates of saving and investment could be forecast to determine the probable amounts of I and S for use in determining the hypothetical *Investment Parity*.

The foregoing is not a definitive analysis. It is merely an attempt to give examples of "normal" relationships which presumably must exist in the price, wage, income, saving, and investment structure. Such indexes were not needed in a free market price system. The price system determined the proper relationships through the free competitive action of demand and supply. When an economy like ours has departed substantially from the free market as the balancing device, it sometimes works so poorly that there must be an alternative. We say vaguely that the alternative is planning. But, in this sense, what is planning? It is not simply regulation. The Wilsonian question arises, regulation for what? If it is regulation for balance, then there must be some theoretical basis for determining what constitutes balance. The definitive answer cannot be given here, but we can point out (1) that the theory of balance in a nonmarket economy can be worked out; (2) that it will consist of a theory of the relationships between prices, incomes, savings, and investment needed for full employment and rapid economic growth; and (3) that it must be applied in a concentrated corporate capitalist system through a form of informational planning if balance and growth are to be maintained.

In discussing economic measures of balance, one must not lose sight of the broader social outlook of Galbraith, to the effect that a social balance is needed between government and private expenditures, between physical goods and services, between welfare and social expenditures on material things, and between investment in physical and human capital. But here again, although the goals are admirable, they cannot mean very much as long as they are left vague and undefined. We need parity measures of the rapidity of growth of education over the growth of, let us say, investment in new steel capacity. We are inclined to say that such matters can only be decided in a political or arbitrary fashion. But there may be "laws" of social growth which we could accept for a given stage in the advancing wealth of an economy. In a war, both guns and butter are important. Because the decision between them is forced on us in a war, we think about the matter and arrive at a ratio that seems reasonable. In peace, automobiles and classrooms are both important. Since the free market can give us no answer as to the relative value of each, we relegate the decision to politics instead of working out a socioeconomic theory of the proper relation between them. In other words, we prefer politics to rationality. The result is lack of balance. Planning means balance. Balance requires theory. We cannot reach social balance without planning. Thus, social balance requires a theory of social balance. It cannot be left merely in the state of a vague social ideal. Formulae must be worked out.

(6) *Planning Goals*. There has been no more enlightened approach since his day than the approach of Wilson to the problems resulting from the decline of competition. This can be said because the great corporation, although it revolutionized capitalism, did not cause a "revolution." We remained in capitalism. Since the essence of capitalism was economic balance through the free market, the decline or elimination of the market threatened the survival of capitalism unless alternative effective means of balance could be found. Wilson's solution was the intervention of government to restore freedom and the market where this was possible. But since it was largely impossible, the intervention should also be directed toward *the establishment through government of the effects or results of the free market*. In other words, classicism was largely discarded as a control device *but it remained as an ideal or body of goals*. It is here contended that there are probably no other goals possible under capitalism. If we prefer other goals, we should change to fascism or communism.

The basic goals of capitalism are balance, growth, efficiency, freedom, and equality. Related to these is the basic goal of greater and greater production, but production need not be defined merely as production of material things. It includes services, both individual and social. There is no inconsistency between the expansion of automobile production and the expansion of college education under capitalism. Both are expressions of belief in growth, efficiency, balance, freedom and equality. In capitalist planning, therefore, the goals of economic life are already outlined. It remains only to define, make specific, enlarge, and interpret these five objectives. For example, many questions arise concerning any one of them, such as efficiency. Is it efficient in the use of labor to displace it through automation and at the same time provide no alternative uses for it? Is it efficient and productive of growth in the long run to devote research funds primarily to applied science to the neglect of pure science? In other words, what does efficiency really mean in terms of mid-twentieth century capitalism where the free market does not give us many of the answers?

(7) *Controls and Regulation.* Since the Civil War, economic control in various forms has grown steadily. We began by abandoning free trade. The rise of monopoly and oligopoly meant increasing private control over prices and output. The rise of unions meant control over wages. The farm programs resulted in control over farm prices. Governments at all levels stepped in to introduce a great variety of controls over business practices, the quality of goods, credit and money, prices in agriculture and public utilities, and the overall level of spending. In more recent years, the huge defense program has become a very important regulatory factor in the volume and nature of private production and employment. Regulation is not new. Absolute laissez-faire has never existed and laissez-faire in a substantial degree died long before the New Deal. The New Dealers merely celebrated its delayed funeral, and thus shocked thousands of economic mystics who believed that somehow, somewhere, it was still alive.

The growth and extent of control is understandable and not cause for alarm. Furthermore, control is likely to increase whether any of the planning proposals made here are ever adopted. In American corporate capitalism, there is no choice between control and lack of control. There is only a choice between kinds and degrees of control. As we have said earlier, there is also no choice between planning and lack of planning. We already have planning and it is with us to stay. Here again, choice centers around kinds and degrees. What is proposed is further centralization of planning, but centralization requires some increase in the centralization of regulation and control. It is unrealistic to assume that we can get overall direction in our economy through information, leadership and guidance alone. In connection with the type of planning proposed, therefore, it becomes necessary to visualize possible increased controls.

Since one of the major goals of capitalism is freedom, the controls must be of such a nature as to provide the maximum freedom consistent with economic balance, efficiency, growth, and equality. The desire for freedom, and our belief in its economic value, have explained our preference for indirect economic control through taxes, spending, interest rates, bank policy, and tariffs. But these older controls were not only indirect, but, in a sense, peripheral. The center of the economic system has always been the price-wage structure. It has been regarded as sacrosanct, and as untouchable by government control except in war or in the case of farmers, or in the case of businesses regarded as public utilities. *It must now be entered, but in a way which will leave the major decisions still in the hands of business and labor and which will retain the maximum degree of freedom.* And it must be entered primarily to promote balance and *to protect the general or national interest.*

In suggesting peacetime controls, there would seem to be two possibilities, which might be called the *limited or leadership approach* and the *public utility approach.*

The limited leadership approach has evolved in the Kennedy and Johnson administrations. It is a new device to bring balance into the economy and can be attributed in part to the revival of intellectualism in Washington, the first since the early years of the New Deal. In general, it consists of establishing guide lines which will reveal the public interest, and in providing standby executive powers to use fiscal and monetary policy and tariff changes as means of preventing depression and inflation. As yet, these approaches are not very well defined, and are meeting with strong opposition from the leaderships of large unions and large corporations. It may be possible to read too much into the Kennedy and Johnson proposals and to falsely anticipate their full development. It is too early to make any predictions as to how these suggested techniques will evolve or whether they will fall victim to the pressures of both big business and big labor.

If they were comprehensively developed and made the control mechanism of a national planning program, however, they might very well provide the basis for successful capitalistic planning. As we have said, they are guide lines and standby powers. But what is really meant? The Kennedy Administration was not too sure. As we interpret them, guide lines could mean two things: (a) indications of price, wage, and output policies which are in the general interest and violation of which would suffer from adverse public opinion; and (b) the actual setting of maximum and minimum prices and wages in given fields. They can thus be suggested specific results for bargaining or the setting of upper and lower bargaining limits. To propose either specific results or limits has already been attacked as an interference with freedom, but it may be necessary if the public interest is to be protected against self-interested power groups in both business and labor.

The enforcement of the guide lines will come either from the pressure of public opinion supporting the Federal Government, or through standby powers which can be invoked when the guide lines are ignored. In addition to the setting up of guide lines proposed by the Kennedy and Johnson Administrations, the President might be empowered to impose compulsory arbitration in the case of wage disputes, and to fix prices or even nationalize industries in cases of flagrant violation of the public interest. The Federal Government already has the power to compel postponement of strikes for a period of eighty days in disputes which create a national emergency. This power could be extended to allow the Federal Government to impose compulsory arbitration as a last defense of the public interest. The power could be applied not only to defense industry but to any industry regarded as basic to the economy, such as steel or automobile manufacture, and in situations of economic stalemate which seriously injure thousands of persons not directly involved in the disputes.

The establishment of guide lines which would be enforceable by standby powers would have meaning and strength only if they were related to a national master plan arrived at through the system of democratic planning described above. The establishment of guide lines in a piecemeal and specialized manner and defended as necessary for the public interest without being first related to a national economic plan, and after specific disputes have arisen, is both weak and dangerous. This is so because the basis of acceptance by the parties involved, both corporations and unions, has not been prepared for by democratic advance planning. Resistance and cries of discrimination are inevitable under these circumstances. Danger arises also from distortion by applying guide lines in a specialized manner. If a national plan existed, however, and the guide lines were justifiable derivatives, not only would adherence be more likely, but strong measures of enforcement such as fixing of maximum prices, postponement of strikes and compulsory arbitration would be more readily accepted. Taxation, spending, and credit control standby powers could also be more intelligently applied.

A more extreme approach is the creation of public utilities. A public utility is a business "affected with a public interest." But in actual practice there is a great deal of opinion and tradition involved, and there is a misconception that all public utilities are "natural" monopolies. Why are electric, telephone, gas, water, and transportation businesses regarded as public utilities while steel, aluminum, automobiles, cement and meat packing are not? Certainly not because all the public utilities are natural monopolies. The main reasons are that these industries serve vital needs and have traditionally been regulated. It has occurred to many people, however, that the steady functioning of the steel and automobile industries at reasonable levels of prices and output may be almost as important as the provision of electricity and telephone service. Our key industries are all affected with a public interest. It is only a matter of degree. If there is no other effective means of maintaining growth and balance in concentrated corporate capitalism, the extreme solution would be to declare all the major industries public utilities and have them regulated by utility commissions according to policies set down in a national economic plan. Unless the power problem can be solved in some other way, we should be prepared to take this step. The industries which are now public utilities have prospered and have not suffered unduly from public regulation. The essentials of capitalism have been preserved. The utility commission has substituted for a free market that had disappeared long before the utility commissions were created.

Public utility regulation, of course, has been subjected to a variety of criticisms in the last fifty years. It is claimed that utility commissions are often composed of uninformed political appointees; that they favor and protect the utilities rather than the public; that rate-fixing based on the original or reproduction cost theories has proved unworkable because of delay and difficulty in arriving at utility capital valuations; that there is no answer to the question of what is a fair return; and that some fields have been held back through inadequate returns to the benefit of other fields (railroads versus buses and airlines). But there is no movement for the abolition of public utility regulation. The situation in these fields is infinitely better than it would have been without regulation. Moreover, some of the weaknesses of utility regulation may be attributed to lack of broad national planning concerning the growth of power resources and transportation. If public utility regulation were more widely used and related to national planning, it would be more effective and defensible.

It is our belief that broad use of public utility regulation based on an attempt to maintain the price relations (price equals cost plus a fair profit) that would result from a free market is logically related to Wilson's philosophy and his approach to the power problem. If one believes, as he did, in a *regularized* restoration of the operation of "natural" economic laws to an economic system which has forsaken the free market, the public utility type of regulation which attempts to establish the results of the free market seems the logical solution. Moreover, this solution is consistent with belief in freedom since it established more of a *regularization* than a regulation of price policy. In a sense, utility commissions do not *regulate* prices. The utility has great latitude in suggesting price changes and can oppose the commission. What the commission does is to set up rules for the price-fixing process, relate them to economic theory, and insist that they be followed. The rules may be wrong and the economics obsolete, but at least there is regularity and a consideration of the public interest.

SUMMARY

To sum up the preceding pages, the economic solutions of the American power problem are (a) the strengthening of older solutions, and (b) the development of a new form of capitalist economic planning directed by the Federal Government. The older solutions consist of the use of the antitrust laws, the regulation of competition through the Federal Trade Commission, fiscal policy, economic pluralism, consumer representation, and the promotion of competition.

Of the older solutions, the planned and conscientious use of fiscal policy to restore and maintain economic balance is of greatest value and significance. Together with capitalist planning it can go far toward meeting the problems of power in our economic life. Capitalist planning consists of a further centralization of the planning which already pervades large corporate enterprise and government. These needs for central coordination have resulted from the abandonment of the free market and the growth of large corporate power concentrates. The methods of planning should be informational and democratic. Planning policy should be the responsibility of a National Planning Board on which the President's Council of Economic Advisers, an industry planning board, and labor and consumers should be represented. The task of drawing up national "five year plans" should be assigned to the President's Council of Economic Advisers, assisted by a large research staff. Ultimate approval of the plans by the public should be obtained through congressional ratification.

Implementation of the plans should be achieved mainly through the leadership of the Federal Government and the cooperation of the various basic economic groups. But some regulation should be introduced. In the first instance, this might take the form of guide lines of policy, consisting largely of ceilings and floors for wages and prices. If adherence to the plans cannot be achieved by these processes and the power problem becomes acute, it will be necessary to consider the possibility of declaring all major businesses public utilities and regulating them in the public interest and on the basis of modern economic theory as related to a national economic plan.

XII

Governmental and Social Solutions of the Power Problem

THE establishment of a system of national planning, or, in fact, the achievement of any national goals requires political organization. But the ease of political organization varies directly with the extent to which a purpose can be personalized. It is easy to get voters aroused when an issue is closely related to individual experiences. During the great depression, the plight of the unemployed, the small businessmen, and the farmers was close at hand, and the rapid deterioration of the economic situation needed little illustration. As a result, Franklin Roosevelt had no great difficulty in organizing the Grand Alliance that swept him into office in 1932 and reelected him three times. When a public purpose is impersonal and cannot be easily connected with John Jones across the street who has been out of work for months, and Henry Smith whose hardware store just failed down at the corner, the problem of organization is difficult. Such an impersonal purpose is national planning to protect and further the general interest. It is an important purpose, but it is an abstraction. Understanding abstractions is difficult for people who have not had a great deal of education. But it is these very people, the average citizens, who most need to understand and support the general interest, since only through its support can the freedom of the average man be restored.

Another difficulty in organizing politically to promote and protect the general interest is the fact that many deny its existence. They believe that there are only individual and specialized interests. Society is merely a matter of compromises between conflicting special interests and a general interest surmounting other interests is regarded as fictitious. Lack of basic understanding of the origins of American democracy makes this misconception not only possible, but widespread, among large self-oriented segments of our society.

Another difficulty with the general interest as a political objective is preoccupation with ourselves as producers. Although economists have often said that production is carried on for the sake of consumption, we place production first because we think that what we consume is dependent on what we "make." But our productive activities are highly specialized and when we concentrate on them, it becomes difficult to think in general interest terms.

Our general interest in the economy is more closely related to consumption than to production. The general interest has been injured in recent years, by inflation and crippling strikes. But both inflation and strikes injure us primarily because we are consumers. We have to pay more than twice as much as we did before the war for steak, furniture, and countless consumer items. In large cities, consumers of bus and subway transportation have been seriously inconvenienced by strikes in these fields. But in each case, the public is not much aroused despite the heavy sacrifices involved. What hurts us as consumers does not seem to matter enough to arouse political action. If our jobs were affected, it would be different. Thus the general interest is often too much of a consumer interest to cause persistent and vigorous political effort on its behalf.

Finally, although the general interest can be personalized

by reference to consumer fraud, exorbitant prices, or twenty blocks walked to work because of a bus strike, it is more an ideological than a personal matter. It means little to most people apart from the specific maladjustments resulting from its neglect except as a broad philosophical point of view concerning a better America. It resembles religious and philosophical issues. *It requires a faith to become politically viable.*

THE NEED FOR LIBERAL LEADERSHIP

Thus a new leadership is required. It is needed to formulate an ideology for a concentrated corporate capitalism that will democratize it and further the general interest. It is needed also to make this ideology politically active by arousing faith in it. Such a leadership can only come from the ranks of American liberals. In our past history, there have been periods of daring liberal leadership. We are entering another period when new, daring intellectual direction is needed.

American liberalism has an intellectual continuity which has not been accompanied by political continuity. Liberal political movements have developed, such as the Progressive Movement, the New Freedom, and the New Deal, and they have died with the death, illness, or rejection of the men who led them. In this respect, we are only to a degree less personal in our politics than Latin Americans. We attach ideas to a personality. When we decide that we no longer like a personality, we discard the ideas also. The Progressive Movement suffered severely when Bryan and Theodore Roosevelt came to be regarded as "dangerous" men. Much of the rejection of Wilson's internationalism was really a rejection of Wilson's alleged austerity, dogmatism, impracticality, and unrealism. Franklin Roosevelt managed to finish his life as a revered personality, but his death made people forget his beliefs and accept in place a vague reverence for his greatness.

Much of the discontinuity of liberalism may also be attributed to reverence for success. Any movement for change, however, cannot count on immediate success unless it quickly triumphs because it is generated by a national crisis, as in the case of the New Deal in 1932. This means that in the absence of such a national crisis, a needed social movement may take years to grow and eventually triumph. In the meantime, its followers must be able to accept periods of defeat and failure. But American liberals are too anxious for immediate success.

Thus American liberalism reveals much political discontinuity. Our liberals often desert their traditions for short-term gains through compromise. They forget that they belong to a tradition which they have inherited in an unbroken line from Jefferson, Madison, Jackson, Lincoln, Bryan, Theodore Roosevelt, Wilson, La Follette, Franklin Roosevelt, Willkie, Truman, Stevenson, Kennedy, and Johnson. The trouble with this tradition, however, is that it has not been consistently and continuously organized, and that it does not lead to a liberal philosophy or ideology which, although constantly revised to suit changing conditions, remains as a *consciously and continuously accepted body of thought* with a large and faithful group of adherents. Liberals are inclined on the one hand, to become compromising and political, or, on the other, to "run when the first shot is fired." Not many American liberals are willing to lose power or a good job for a principle, let alone go to jail for one.

The new liberalism that we need must be idealistic rather than pragmatic. The nature of the new ideology has been previously sketched, but here it is redefined as the modernization of *Wilsonianism*. Basically this means that democracy, viewed as a form of individualism, must be protected and advanced by the Federal Government through the support of the general public. It means that economic and social life should be regulated in order to achieve the effects of the free market and the five goals of capitalism—efficiency, balance, growth, freedom, and equality. It means that the Federal Government should vigorously defend the general interest, and that this interest should be rationally based on a modern economics. It means that individual rights should be protected by law and that, as far as possible, democracy must be restored in our large organic society by internalizing it in the life of the great corporation and the great union. Finally, it means that the need for greater centralization of planning and control through the Federal Government must be recognized. *Having lost freedom from the development of concentrated power, the average man can only regain it by insisting that the Federal Government assume more power, and exercise it through planning for the general interest, which is his interest.* Thus the average man can regain his *freedom only through power,* the power of the Federal Government which presumably he can still control.

It would seem that the liberal voter is in need of the slogan "lest we forget." One is inclined to ask, what was to be gained from the hiatus of the years 1920 to 1932 and 1952 to 1960? Personalities changed in those years and we enjoyed great prosperity, but the evolution of the economy continued toward greater concentration of power and the power problem remained. If one wants to become a conservative, there is no law against it in a free country. But if one is a liberal, there is hardly any reason in supporting Wilson in one election and Harding in the next, or Truman in one election and Eisenhower in the next. The explanation is probably loss of memory. But we can lose memory because what we try to remember may not seem very important. It may not seem significant because it is not really a faith or else it is not really understood. It is paradoxical that in America we have one of the richest and soundest liberal traditions in the

world, but also one of the most fickle and personality conscious liberal voting populations. In what other country
could the desertion of the Democratic party by millions of
supposedly liberal union voters in 1952 be duplicated? Of
course it has been repeatedly said that American unionism
is not ideological. This is considered a virtue. Instead, it is
a serious weakness. The "common sense" of American unionism is long-run bad sense. It is good that labor does not have
a Marxian ideology; but it needs a democratic ideology.

Neither union members nor other parts of the population
can accept the modern democratic ideology without leadership. If the general interest is to be promoted, liberal politicians, corporate executives, union leaders and professional
men must set about seriously and quickly to build a new
liberal philosophy and support it with dedication and courage, regardless of political consequences. There must be a
consciousness of heritage. Liberals made great strides in the
early years of the Wilson Administration. But the movement
was dropped. By 1936, liberals were discarding the liberalism
of the Roosevelt Administration. As things stand, liberals
are overconcerned about the supposed infeasibility of some
of their views. There is a cult of "political infeasibility." In
the liberal's mind today, there are two liberal images: Roosevelt, the father; and Kennedy, the son. Both father and son
were politically minded and politically successful. Unfortunately, it is thought that all liberals must be politically successful even if it requires compromise of principles.

THE DECLINING PUBLIC AND ITS REACTIVATION

Perhaps one of the main hindrances to rational liberalism
in America is the decline of the "public." One need not
accept the extreme position of Mills that we have entered a
mass society, and yet the trend toward "massism" is great.
Advertising and the means of mass communication have
capitalized on the desire for uniformity and conformity re-

sulting from the growing hierarchical nature of our economic and social life and the success of mass production. We are told what to buy over television and radio every hour of the day. We are told what to think by our superiors in the business or union world, by numerous newspaper columnists and by the editorializing of news content in all the media of news. A true "public" is a group of people who get at the facts, react to the views of others through comment and criticism, and make up their minds with a degree of unemotional intellectual independence.

The extent to which we have a true public affects the degree to which democracy can function efficiently. It determines the extent to which the voter can prevent the country from being run by a power élite. In some ways, it is the most important remaining sphere for the operation of individualism. Most of our power and freedom of functioning on an individual basis has been lost in economic life. We still have power as individuals politically. But we seem intent on losing it by rejecting the important art of reading and by avoidance of thought. Instead, we should save our individualism by insistence on knowledge. We should require the radio, press, and television not to treat us as children and to give us facts rather than digests and biased views. Only an active thinking public can secure national policies supporting the average man and the general interest. Part of the solution of the power problem, an important part, is the preservation and activation of a true public.

American government has also suffered for many years from what might be called the "lazy" voter. Presidential elections resemble church attendance on Easter Sunday. Millions go to the polls then and at no other time. Unless we regard the Federal Government as a great corporation controlled by a board of directors and the management during the interim between Presidential elections, we must become more continuously active politically. The interim of relative voter indifference may last eight years, since Presidents are often reelected. Not only should voters be interested in the two-year congressional elections, but in the day-to-day representation of their interests by Congress and the President. And activity does not consist of merely listening to the President's news conference on television or reading the news daily. It is much more than that. The fact that most of us are not continually active politically gives credence to the theory that we are living in a mass society, and that actual control is in the hands of a power élite. Control by a small group of power-motivated men varies inversely with the degree and continuity of the political activity of the individual voters. This is an elementary political truth long recognized by pressure groups.

Although the need for a real public is easy to see, it is difficult to devise means of reactivating the public. The field of political science is full of suggestions. But among the most successful practical means of arousing the voter are discussion groups like the League of Women Voters, and organizations that keep and publicize records of the votes of Congressmen, like the Americans for Democratic Action. The significance of such organizations lies in the fact that the voter must be assisted in getting at the information which is the basis of continuity in political activity. Once armed with the facts, the voter should write letters and send telegrams to congressmen. He should also be active in his local political club.

THE IMPROVEMENT OF CORPORATE AND UNION LEADERSHIP

Our preoccupation with Federal economic planning and fiscal policy and our belief that corporate executives are not yet ready to plan for the whole economy should not be taken as complete rejection of corporate or union leadership. In controlling the leading institutions of our society, their leadership is and will continue to be of great importance.

One further solution of the power problem, therefore, is the improvement and democratization of this leadership.

Improvement of leadership depends in part on the type of leaders selected. In this discussion of the great corporation and the power élite, it was pointed out that selection at the top is not essentially bureaucratic or based on strict principles of merit. The selection is largely based on the qualities of adjustability and acceptability. The result is frequently the selection of cautious and conservative men. The selectees are also organization-oriented and little outside-oriented. The dangers of leadership of this sort, in a technically changing society which needs to be led by intelligent, well-educated, and culturally conscious men with a social morality, are not sufficiently recognized. Ideally, boards of directors should insist on the selection of the latter type of men to head management. In that the management also largely determines its own selection, it should not seek the perpetuation of its own image but a new "social image." Fortunately, there is growing realization of the needs for a new kind of leadership.[1] But the fact that we can still have heads of our greatest corporations who say that the welfare of their particular corporation is the welfare of the country reveals that we are far short of an ideal socialized corporate leadership.

The improvement of corporate leadership means that greater effort should be made to select men who have the following traits: (1) technical competence, (2) managerial competence, (3) judgment, (4) leadership qualities, (5) superior intelligence, (6) knowledge of society, (7) a great sense of social responsibility, (8) a consciousness of and belief in the public consensus, (9) a desire for the formulation of a new corporate ideology and morality, (10) a willingness to participate in a program of broad economic planning centered around the Federal Government, and (11) a desire for innovation and the acceptance of change.

[1] *Cf.* Worthy, J. C., *Big Business and Free Men,* p. 14

Our great corporate executives should be liberals. There is no good reason why they should be conservatives. Many of them are liberals without knowing it. As Worthy has pointed out, the leading business man is likely to be an ". . . innovator. His job, in fact, has been called 'the management of change.' He has much more at stake in the emerging future than in the status quo . . . There is no indication that the rate of change is slowing down; on the contrary it appears to be accelerating. In all this the businessman plays the central role. Whatever else he may be, he is not conservative; in terms of results, 'revolutionary' would be more apt." [1] Business conservatism has been related largely to a struggle for power with unions and the government and opposition to the centralization of control. Contentment with a given power status and recognition of the need for greater centralization should remove much of the justification for conservatism unless one wants to define conservatism merely as identification with big business.

In view of current needs, the quality of union leadership is no more viable than big business leadership. There are at least five union leadership types in existence today, the suspect leadership of Hoffa, the militant, strike-conscious syndicalist leadership of Quill, the collaborationist balance-of-power leadership of Dubinsky, the social and political action leadership of Reuther, and the moderate business unionism of Meany. Every type leaves something to be desired.

As with businessmen, a tentative list of qualities required by the current situation can be made. Thus union leaders need (1) competence in labor-management technology, (2) judgment, (3) leadership talents, (4) superior intelligence, (5) knowledge of society, (6) a great sense of social responsibility, (7) a consciousness of and belief in the public consensus, (8) honesty in the management of membership funds,

1 Worthy, J. C., op. cit., p. 182

(9) belief in and support of the public or general interest as well as union interests, (10) willingness to participate in broad economic planning, and (11) a desire for innovation and acceptance of change. None of the men mentioned has all these qualities but Dubinsky and Reuther come nearest the ideal. Hoffa and Quill are a long way from it.

INTERNALIZING DEMOCRACY

The power problems of our society go beyond the general economic unbalance that we have put in the foreground of the discussion. As has been pointed out, power affects human processes adversely by introducing power motivation and destructive tendencies. It has led also to the violation of basic democratic goals and ideals such as freedom, equality, and the individualism they are based on. In other words, our power problems transcend malfunctioning, crisis, struggle, and disorder. Wilson tried to say this when he described the individual as "swallowed up" by the large corporation, and when he expressed a desire for industrial democracy. To him the effect of power-structuring on the growth of the individual was a very serious matter. Somehow individualism had to be preserved and strengthened in a society organized to thwart it. It was not enough to maintain individualism in political life and in leisure time activities. Individualism had to be retained in productive life.

Another way of expressing this view is to say that democracy must be internalized in the large corporation and the large union. This is a large subject in itself, too large in fact for the scope of this book. We can only suggest some of the broad outlines.

In the large corporation, the internalization of democracy means (1) democratizing corporate leadership and control, (2) developing a new democratic business philosophy, and (3) democratizing employer-employee relationships.

In regard to corporate leadership, the basis of democracy

lies in the attitudes of corporate executives toward their "constituency" which consists of the stockholders, employees, consumers, the local community and the nation. A great deal of thought has been given to possible ways of restoring stockholder control of large corporations. It is impossible to have majority ownership *control* of a large corporation with thousands of stockholders, but it is conceivable that stockholders could exercise greater influence. Among the devices to increase stockholder influence are the elimination of multiple voting for classes of stock, reduction in the use of nonvoting stock, regulations of the Securities and Exchange Commission concerning information furnished when proxies are solicited, and provision of more information to stockholders concerning corporate operations and finances.

Two devices that have proved of some value in recent years are regional stockholders' meetings and small stockholders' committees or representatives. One obstacle to active participation in company affairs is travel. Few stockholders living in California, for example, are willing to travel to a stockholders' meeting in New Jersey unless they have large stock interests. If meetings preliminary to the main meeting, or as substitutes for it, are held in various parts of the country, attendance is much larger and a better cross section of stockholder opinion can be sampled.

Another device, small stockholder representation, has attracted a great deal of publicity. Lewis D. Gilbert, a stockholder in various large corporations, undertook some years ago to solicit the proxies of small stockholders. With these he was able to represent them at the annual meetings of large corporations. Mr. Gilbert raised questions which were of interest to small stockholders, such as the justification for high executive salaries and bonuses, the reasons for not declaring dividends, the level of dividends, and certain specific questions concerning the operations of the companies involved. Among the proposals coming from Gilbert and other small stockholder representatives were adoption of cumulative voting, which is a form of proportional representation; circulation of questionnaires to obtain stockholder opinion; post-meeting reports to stockholders; fuller and more informative annual reports; and preservation of the stockholders' preemptive rights to buy proportionate shares of new stock issues. Still other proposals are greater use of stockholders' suits, stronger state laws regulating corporations, restriction of the use of voting trusts, and even Federal incorporation. Although stockholders may never act effectively to control corporation policy, there is democratic value in giving them as much information as possible, soliciting their opinions in stockholders' meetings, and through questionnaires, and providing them at all times with a "voice." A voice is sometimes almost as important as a controlling vote.

Corporate leadership can be democratized by means other than an increase in stockholder influence. Berle has gone farther than anyone else in making proposals in this direction. He urges (1) a new corporate ideology, (2) adherence to a public consensus or body of morality concerning the modern large corporation, and (3) the legal review of corporate actions which have acquired a political character.

A new morality concerning the behavior of corporations is growing, and there is evidence that corporate executives are increasingly obeying the new morality. The new behavior that will result from these tendencies is not only moral but democratic. Although the corporate élite is never really elected by its constituency, it reacts to the limits set for its activity by the public conscience. But there are other democratic influences at work. These influences are concerned with the philosophy of the corporate executive and his relations with his employees.

THE NEW BUSINESS PHILOSOPHY

As expressed by Worthy, the new business philosophy represents an attempt to get closer to the public and convince them that business is not entirely motivated by self-interest. Ever since the twenties, big business has been aware of the need for good public relations and the education of the public concerning sound business principles. The newness in the current public relations efforts consists in a deeper analysis of the social nature of large corporate business. Perhaps the changing business philosophy can be best illustrated by describing the reasoning of a man like Worthy who is typical of the new social approach.

He believes that businessmen should accept criticism and that criticism is a fundamental aspect of democracy. Business cannot obtain the support of the general public without using public criticism as the basis of a new personal integrity. A climate of opinion favorable to business depends on business integrity. High-powered salesmenship to promote public acceptance of business is not as effective as the experiences the public has with good business practices or business ethics revealed through deeds rather than words. As he puts it, "the American way of life does not need to be *sold* so much as it needs to be *lived*. . . . Business must also conform with and aid in strengthening the basic values of American society, which are strongly democratic." [1]

The main defect of American business ideology, he asserts, is its foundation on the principle of self-interest. "The ". . . avowal of self interest . . . renders the businessman and the business system forever suspect." [2] Self-interest runs counter to Christian ethics, and although a capitalist business system, operating on self-interest, may be more humane than other economic systems which claim to be for the general

[1] Worthy, *op. cit.*, p. 15
[2] *Ibid.*, p. 23

welfare, it is not as defensible. The public takes business at its word, and assumes that only selfish motives underly business activity. In times of crisis, the public refuses to turn to business for leadership because it fears that business will not work for the general interest. All this must be changed, according to Worthy, by reworking the concept of self-interest. The majority of the public no longer accepts the view of Adam Smith that self-interest through an "invisible hand" promotes the general interest.

Reworking the concept of self-interest involves the realization that business is actually motivated by human impulses in addition to self-interest. "In business there has always been a system of human relations as well as a system of economic relations." [1] Business men also play "multiple rather than unitary roles." [2] They are not only business men, but participants in other forms of social life not entirely connected with business gain. Also, in the reworking of the self-interest concept, emphasis must be given to underlying moral motivation. Although businessmen are interested in profits, their profit-making efforts are guided and restrained by strong moral beliefs based on Judeo-Christian ethics. "These values find expression in business life—incompletely and unevenly, perhaps, but in an appreciable degree." [3] Ethical values have been stressed in the development of management as a semi-profession. Thus, self-interest can be regarded as a reflection of a moral code if it is self-interest to act ethically. The strengthening of this code, and universal adherence to it by businessmen, would make the business system conform to the needs of human welfare although apparently self-motivated.

Reworking self-interest requires still another element ac-

1 *Ibid.*, p. 28
2 *Ibid.*, p. 30
3 *Ibid.*, p. 33

cording to Worthy, a new view or theory of enterprise based upon the true nature of the large corporation. The great corporate business changed the role of profits and created a new profession of management. Due to the separation of ownership from management ". . . the managers of the corporation cannot be said to be actuated by a profit motive in the classical sense because of their relatively small ownership." [1] Thus, self-interest loses its narrow profit-seeking meaning, and involves the new motives of obtaining position, status, and responsibility in the corporation. Since these motives dominate management, business motivation is really concerned with the welfare and continuity of the business. Profit-seeking is not for selfish reasons, but for the survival of the business, and the survival of large productive corporations is in the general interest. Thus, the motives of businessmen are actually directed in part toward the general interest. As Worthy puts it, "A more realistic and more defensible doctrine of profits will have to be built around the survival needs of the enterprise as an instrumentality of social service." [2]

Corporate enterprise, as Worthy and other liberal businessmen realize, brought into existence a "profession" of management. Professional management meant the direction of business by men who acted as trustees, were concerned with service, and thought in terms of continuity, stable profits, and long-range planning. Management began to realize that its business responsibilities were also social responsibilities. According to Worthy, "Unless the policies of business—especially big business—benefit society they will not in the long run benefit business. . . . Socially irresponsible action is also economically irresponsible action—and vice versa." And he adds that "it is the obligation of managers to protect and serve

1 *Ibid.*, p. 36
2 *Ibid.*, p. 39

the public interest, not as a fortuitous by-product but as an integral part of their managerial function." [1]

Management has also developed a more socialized outlook because of factors related to the character of their employees. Worthy contends that employers in America have greater sensitivity and diffidence in dealing with their employees than their counterparts in other countries. This he attributes to the equalitarian traditions of the United States, where authority cannot be readily exercised over men regarded as equal in social or political status to the boss. Once immigrant laborers were replaced by second generation "Americans," equality of status had to be granted and authority exercised with due respect for the worker. In addition, the organization of unions enforced a more "respectful" attitude on the employers. Another factor involved was the persistent scarcity of labor. Anything scarce must be valued and respected. Underlying these influences toward greater responsibility to labor was the social philosophy in America of "living better." Businessmen wanted a better way of life, not only for themselves, but for the rest of American society.

The reworking of the concept of self-interest or the development of a new social philosophy of enterprise will inevitably serve to democratize business leadership. By democratization is meant here greater sensitivity to criticism, greater sense of responsibility to the business constituency, and in general, a greater concern for the public interest. The influence of the changes in business philosophy in democratizing corporate leadership must not be underestimated.

DEMOCRATIZING THE JOB: FREEDOM WITHIN ENTERPRISE

Many years have passed since liberals first began to complain that the individual had lost his individuality in the giant corporation. Since those days, concern for the growth and freedom of the individual in economic life has either

1 *Ibid.*, p. 41

dimmed or has become part of the current preoccupation with employer-employee relations. The basic threat to democracy in the frustration of individual growth and freedom does not now attract much attention. But the most important part of the life of an American is still his work life. If this is authoritarian, uninteresting, unchallenging, and frustrating to personal growth, his way of living is not only unpleasant and undemocratic, but is wasteful of his potential contribution to productive effort. An authoritarian power system developed through the pyramidal organization of the large corporation can destroy democracy during the eight hours of the working day for millions of people.

Both Berle and Worthy have pointed out that the large business is partly political in nature, and all business, as viewed from the human relations standpoint, is a form of political economy. Berle has described the large corporation as a great political system in which executives are accountable to a constituency consisting of stockholders, workers, consumers, and the general public. Thus, *externally* the corporation is a form of government. But Worthy has added that *internally* a business is a form of government.[1]

The American tradition is one of freedom and democracy. But freedom can no longer be achieved through laws forbidding restraint. Positive freedom is required not only through government, but business action also. As Worthy expresses it, "Freedom is no longer merely a matter of governmental policy; it is now a matter of business policy as well. . . . We cannot have a democratic society if so large a section as that represented by industry is run in an authoritarian manner. Business, in the way it is run, can support and strengthen democracy or seriously undermine it." [2] The inconsistency between our democratic principles and our concern for free enterprise *outside* of business in market free-

[1] *Ibid.*, p. 53
[2] *Ibid.*, p. 54

dom and freedom from government control, and the authoritarian *internal* organization of many large corporations disturbs Worthy. To him ". . . one of the ironies of modern times is the failure to see the full implications of the free enterprise system for the internal conduct of business affairs." [1] Thus we need freedom *within* enterprise for a full democratic life.

Apart from the importance of freedom *per se,* the internalizing of freedom in corporate organization may actually be conducive to a considerable increase in efficiency. Authoritarianism, hierarchy, centralization, and rigid and detailed control in large businesses are usually justified on the ground that technology requires this sort of organization. Worthy and a number of other writers on management, however, have denied this. Authoritarianism, and the accompanying rigid organizational features of large businesses, over-functionalization, and over-centralization, cause inefficiency. Undoubtedly these organizational concepts have often been carried beyond the point where they increase efficiency. Less organization and more democracy through defunctionalization and decentralization may promote efficiency. Of course, a strong desire for freedom within enterprise may lead one to exaggerate the possibilities of increasing efficiency by democracy through organizational changes. But these possibilities are only beginning to be explored by liberal executives and it is too early to go to the opposite extreme and deny that they exist.

Whether authoritative organization can be replaced by democratic organization or not, its adverse effects are fairly obvious. Where authority rather than individual initiative and responsibility are relied upon, many detailed controls must be introduced, and a large controlling staff set up. As a result, there are human losses consisting of apathy, lack of initiative, and limitations on individual growth, adaptability,

[1] *Ibid.,* p. 55

and the development of problem-solving ability. Also, an anti-management psychology often develops. Men feel that they are merely parts of a great machine, and that they are considered only as means to ends and not as ends in themselves. In these circumstances, men resist the organization unless they can be converted into indoctrinated and obedient robots.

As a consequence of the kind of authoritarian economic world in which many of us live, two kinds of comments are heard. On the one hand, employers say, "You cannot get a conscientious worker nowadays. They care about their paychecks rather than the job and seldom give an honest day's work." On the other hand, employees say, "A man who has an interesting job is one in a million. One must not expect an interesting job. I can't wait to get home from work so that I can really live again." What both are really saying is that the concentration of power is destroying the life of the individual. Liberal businessmen like Worthy realize this. In his words, "When the methods of business organization increase the psychological dependency of its members—workers and executives alike—they hinder the processes of individual growth and development basic to democracy. . . . We need to acknowledge that the purpose of a human organization, whether business or otherwise, can only be defined in terms of the people in it." [1] Business, he contends, has created a problem of frustration in individual development and only business can solve it. But will it?

When there is a problem, it is satisfying to find some one person, practice, or theory that is at fault. Liberal businessmen are inclined to blame the overcentralized and functionalized organization of large business on Frederick W. Taylor, the American father of scientific management. No doubt many excesses can be blamed on Taylor. He had a profound influence on business organization, and used engineering

1 *Ibid.*, p. 59

techniques excessively in dealing with management problems. As a result, management became overmechanical. A large human machine was built up to parallel and control the large plant or physical machine. Men were adapted to mechanisms rather than mechanisms to men. In many fields, the mechanisms rapidly replaced the men and are still replacing them. Large corporations have been primarily concerned with production and machines. They are interested in function rather than the men who function.

OVERFUNCTIONALIZATION

Taylor had tremendous influence in promoting *functionalization* in business organization. This consisted of grouping functions according to technical similarity. Its objects were to increase workers' skill and improve supervision. All lathe, drill-press, and milling-machine workers were grouped together in separate administrative units. Functional supervision accompanied all phases of work, giving rise to functional bosses concerned with time cards, work inspection, materials flow, discipline, and so forth. This was carrying over the detailed specialization of physical processes into management with the resulting detailed specialization of planning, supervision, and control. Human factors such as thought and initiative were transferred from workers to management until only a handful of men knew what the whole organization was about, and exercised the higher functions of thought and creativity.

With modern technology a great deal of functionalization was inevitable, but it has been overdone. As a result, people have been dealt with not as flesh and blood human beings, but as productive units grouped in categories as to status and function. Thought, initiative, responsibility, control, planning, imagination, creativity, understandng, and, in fact, most of the mental aspects of participation in business processes have been shifted to the higher management levels.

"The process," says Worthy, "has been fantastically wasteful for industry and society. . . . Much of the difficulty lies in the fact that industry, following the tenets of scientific management, has systematically deprived workers of the real and effective participation in industry."[1]

Worthy is concerned about two other results of Taylorism. In the first place, functionalization greatly complicated the problems of coordination and control. Since responsibility and initiative were taken away from workers and the lower levels of the supervisory personnel, the upper controlling staff had to be greatly enlarged and an increasing number of control problems handled toward the top of the organization. Specialization in general creates the problem of coordination, and as specialization increases, the need for coordination increases. But specialization may reach a point where the greater efficiency at the work bench is offset by the growing cost of the supervisory staff needed.

In the second place, Worthy is concerned over the growth of planning. At least his is a consistent position. Many businessmen approve of a high degree of planning so long as it is *business* planning. But they are inconsistent in supporting business planning as a great good and attacking government planning as the very essence of evil. Worthy attacks both forms of planning. Failure, however, to extend planning to the whole economy to a greater degree than is now the case causes tendencies toward economic and social unbalance since neither the free market nor group competition can serve as completely effective balancing factors. Reduction of business planning through defunctionalization may have human advantages but it will not, as Worthy supposes, remove the need for overall economic planning. The fact that departments are set up in a business to act independently because they deal with a whole process or product rather than with one function in an interrelated process has no bearing

[1] *Op. cit.,* pp. 70-71

on the problems of unduly high wages or prices in the industry involved.

Planning has many aspects that may be unrelated. Thus, the reduction of production planning will not necessarily reduce price planning. Planning is not an epidemic disease which if not controlled in one area will spread to another. There is no simple causal connection as follows: Taylorism caused production planning. Production planning causes market and price planning. Business price and production planning causes government planning. Government planning causes communism. Frederick W. Taylor is the main cause of communism! Taylor may have stifled human initiative, but he will never be buried in the Kremlin wall.

OVERCENTRALIZATION OF PRODUCTION

Closely related to overfunctionalization is overcentralization. The high degree of specialization in management resulting from overfunctionalization means that organizations become much larger and that control gravitates to fewer hands at higher levels. The organization structure becomes a large pyramid with many hierarchical layers of administration, formal controls replacing face-to-face relations, and the growth of both "social" and "administrative" distance. As Worthy has pointed out "... functionalization has the inevitable effect of increasing the size of the administrative unit and making effective decentralization impossible beyond the point in the organization structure where the process of functionalization begins." [1]

The *well-rounded* use of human capacity varies inversely with the size of an organization. For this reason thousands of people today would rather work for a small organization, even at a lower salary, than for a large organization. The persistence of thousands of unprofitable small farms and businesses is partly due to distaste for size or to working for

[1] *Op. cit.,* pp. 90-91

others. In a small business, each position is less specialized. There is far greater expression of the whole personality. Opportunity exists to assume responsibility and exercise initiative. There is a close personal relationship of a face-to-face character among the workers and between them and the boss. If the personnel involved are congenial, the work life can be a good life which satisfies a variety of psychological impulses and promotes individual development. The growth of bigness and the centralization of power are matters of concern because of the maladjustments and problems they create for society as a whole, but they are also equally of concern because of the problems they create for the growth and happiness of the individual.

Thus, society seems to be faced with a dilemma. As Worthy says, there is "... on the one hand, the tendency of technological change to foster the growth of large organizations and, on the other, the evil consequences attendant on such growth." [1] But Worthy is optimistic. He believes that the dilemma is more apparent than real and that through administrative reorganization of large businesses, small units can be created within them that resemble small businesses. These smaller units will restore not only some of the advantages of individual expression and growth characteristic of small businesses, but greater efficiency and the fuller use of human capacities as well.

Worthy's solution is a shift in organization from a functional to a purpose or product basis. He says that much of the vast scale of organization is a result "... not so much of economic and technical factors as of the unhappy and often unnecessary principle of functional organization." [2] Also at fault is the theory of the limited span of control. The English writer on management, Lyndall Urwick, insisted that one man could not supervise effectively more than a dozen

[1] *Ibid.*, p. 90
[2] *Ibid.*, pp. 98-99

subordinates; that to increase the span of control beyond this number would result in overwork and inefficiency on the part of the executive. The solution in the event of a greater number of subordinates was "layering," or the building up of the organization vertically through the additions of layers of administration in a hierarchical pyramid.

But the "layering" has serious disadvantages. It creates "administrative distance" and greater problems of communication. It distorts perspective. Before the top administrator gets the facts about an administrative situation upon which he must pass judgment, they have been sifted by several subordinates in succeeding levels below him, through whom they have passed. Other difficulties develop. Lower executives have a hard time identifying with the top leadership because of the remoteness of the top of the organization. Also, it becomes an effort to make changes and introduce new ideas. A highly layered vertical organization creates status positions at the various administrative levels. Reputations must be protected. A mistake is covered up as long as possible. A new idea cannot come from a lower level lest it question the competence of the men at the next highest levels.

The way out of these difficulties involves the establishment of flatter or more horizontal organization structures with broader spans of control. In other words, there must be greater decentralization. But broader spans are possible only "... if the work of subordinates can be made *less* interlocking and *less* interdependent." [1] In other words, decentralization is dependent upon less functionalization. It is dependent also on the possibility of decentralizing responsibility. The men in charge of the decentralized units must be capable of making decisions and exercising initiative. Only their ability will make it possible for an organization to function well when supervision has been reduced to a minimum.

[1] *Ibid.*, p. 105

But the results of such a decentralization are not only the elimination of the disadvantages of layering. The most important results concern the individual. The executives and the workers in the smaller units have greater opportunity to experience the personal advantages of small business. As Worthy puts it, one of the root problems of modern business organization is that ". . . people have been so hemmed in by supervision and controls that they have too little opportunity to move ahead on their own." Loosely knit organization structures are good because of ". . . the superior opportunities they provide for personal growth." [1] He adds that this ". . . type of organization structure and executive leadership . . . compares closely with basic characteristics of American society." [2]

CONCLUSIONS

There may be great unexplored possibilities for the increase of individual action and responsibility within the large corporate structure. The growth of participation in the control by both the rank and file of employees and the stockholders is necessary for the democratization of the American economic system. Despite the failure thus far to develop these possibilities, one may conclude, however, that even with their full development, our power problems would not be wholly solved. In the end, the hierarchical influence of modern technology will dominate. We cannot, in view of the technological tendencies toward greater power structuring, expect to see much return in our economic system toward the personality-expanding influences of small business units.

The protection and promotion of individualism will have to come mainly through the action of individuals in their capacity as voters, and through the development of a new liberal movement which will promote the general interest.

[1] *Ibid.*, pp. 110-111
[2] *Ibid.*, p. 118

The welfare of Americans as *individuals* is linked to the general interest, and not to their special interests as producers. Only through support of the general interest by a new liberal philosophy which advocates further centralization of economic planning can our power problems be solved.

Afterword

IN THE preceding pages, a journey was made through American history from the days of Hamilton and Jefferson to the current era of Kennedy and Johnson. In it, we have been concerned about the welfare of the individual or common man, his needs for freedom and self-development. We have been concerned about democracy because in essence democracy consists of this freedom of the individual It is not mere majority rule or a form of paternalism on the common man's behalf. No matter what the aims or the political structure of society, democracy does not really exist unless there is both positive and negative freedom for the individual.

In our journey we saw that democracy and freedom were approximately achieved in a world of equality and no power. Had this classical world of no power ever fully developed, and had it been allowed to continue in existence unthreatened by destructive social changes, the issues we have discussed would never have arisen. But the classical world of the small independent farmers, merchants, and manufacturers was largely destroyed by the growth of industrialism and large corporations which concentrated power, both political and economic, in the hands of a few, and by the rise of dynamic materialism which subordinated equality and freedom as American goals.

In our journey we also saw that the individual revolted against his loss of power. At the beginning of American history, the small men who were mainly farmers struggled successfully against the encroachment of industrialism. The power struggle was a group struggle of the small men against the rising industrialists. But the Civil War turned over the Federal Government to the representatives of business, and in the years after the war, industrialism and the concentration of corporate power grew rapidly. A second phase in the struggle for power began, in which individuals, again mainly farmers, sought to protect their freedom by recapturing the Federal Government and by anti-railroad, antitrust, and cheap money legislation. They sought to curb, regulate, and destroy the corporate power concentrates, and restore the free competitive world of no power. Their efforts had little success. They were able to regulate the railroads, but could not obtain cheap money or destroy the trusts. Except for the first two years of the Wilson Administration, little constructive legislation was passed on behalf of the small man and the general interest. Moreover, no socioeconomic theory developed which would explain the new power-structured society and provide solutions for the power problem the small man faced. No new ideology appeared which could serve as a protection for the freedom of the individual in an age of power. There were only Theodore Roosevelt's *New Nationalism,* a form of state paternalism, and Wilson's *New Freedom,* which sought to regulate business in such a way as to restore the results of competitive enterprise. Both were promptly forgotten during the prosperous years after World War I.

The Great Depression crisis of 1929 found us unprepared in theory and ideology. The Depression, however, restored the small man to power in Washington through the *Grand*

Alliance led by Franklin Roosevelt. But without either a new socioeconomic theory or an ideology based on new theory, the New Deal experimented with new approaches and relied heavily on the "need" philosophy and paternalism of unintellectual social workers. It finally succeeded in bringing recovery through deficit spending. Having successfully doctored the economy by this method, New Dealers were pleased to discover that they had followed some aspects of the economics of J. M. Keynes.

But the Dealers were primarily interested in recovery, relief, and reform rather than in the restoration of democracy and individualism. As a result of the doctrine of countervailing power and their desire to organize labor and other social groups, they succeeded in increasing rather than decreasing the concentration of power. They converted the power struggle into a dangerous competition between power groups without providing any means of protecting the general interest. They provided the common man with a pragmatic, unintellectual, political leadership in place of the intellectualism of Wilson. They were closer in viewpoint to the Progressives than they were to the *New Freedom*.

The solution of the power problem, we have seen, must be based on an intellectual, ideological, general interest type of leadership. It requires a new socioeconomic theory, a new ideology, and a new body of ethics. In our attempt to draw the broad outlines of the needed new ideological foundation for our current power-structured society, we have pointed to two basic facts. First, the present most urgent power problem has become one of economic unbalance due to inflation in a relatively affluent society. Keynesian economics provides no solution because of the power-pressured upwriting of the price-wage fabric. This is the economic fact. In addition, we find ourselves in a society in which the leading corporate executives, the top military men, the union leaders, and a small group of leading politicians exercise enormous concentrated power. They come close to constituting a power élite which controls Congress and the voting public. This is the second, or political, fact.

Freedom was lost by the average man when power became concentrated in the hands of a few during the period from 1870 to 1930. There was one basic way of regaining freedom. The individual had lost his power because of the loss of equality resulting from the concentration of power. Thus *the only way the common man could restore his freedom was through power. He had to get his equality back, and he could retrieve it only by taking power away from the leaders of the power concentrates.* La Follette and the liberals needed to destroy the power concentrates or take away their power through public regulation. If a free, no-power economy could have been created, the common man would have gotten his power back because of the resumption of equality. His freedom would have been reestablished *through power,* first by obtaining political power and then by taking the power of the great concentrates and diffusing it among the millions of small men.

But freedom through power now requires a different method. If the liberals and progressives had gained full political power in 1880, 1890, or even 1900, they might have restored free competition. Whether or not this was possible before World War I, it is impossible today to create a universal system of free competition. Concentration of power has become so pervasive and efficient that it cannot be removed. *Freedom through power now requires the common man to gain control of the Federal Government and extend its power through greater planning and control over the power concentrates.* Economic power cannot be destroyed by the political power exercised by the common man. It is too late. The only road to freedom is through the extension of the power of the Federal Government acting in behalf of the common man and the general interest, which is also his interest.

To achieve this end, the common man must understand it. To understand it, he must be led by those who understand it. Then he must consistently and vigorously exercise his great political power to gain and retain control of the Federal Government. But if this control is to be used to plan the economy, the planning must be based on sound socioeconomic theory and a general interest ideology. Without these, the planning will fail and the chance of the common man to regain his freedom may be lost forever.

Selected Bibliography

Beard, Charles and Mary, *The Rise of American Civilization,* Macmillan, New York, 1930.

Berle, Adolf, Jr., *The Twentieth Century Capitalist Revolution,* Harcourt Brace, New York, 1954.

Berle, Adolf, Jr., *Power without Property,* Harcourt Brace, New York, 1959.

Berle, Adolf, Jr., and Means, Gardiner, *The Modern Corporation and Private Property,* Macmillan, New York, 1932.

Beveridge, W. H., *Full Employment in a Free Society,* Norton, New York, 1945.

Buchanan, Scott, *The Corporation and the Republic,* Fund for the Republic, New York, 1958.

Burns, Arthur Robert, *The Decline of Competition,* McGraw-Hill, New York, 1936.

Carey, H. C., *Principles of Political Economy,* N. Kelley, New York.

Chandler, Lester V., *Inflation in the United States, 1940-1948,* Harper and Bros., New York, 1951.

Croly, Herbert, *The Promise of American Life,* Macmillan, New York, 1909.

Dewey, John, *Freedom and Culture,* Putnam, New York, 1939.

Douglas, William O., *Democracy and Finance,* Yale University Press, New Haven, 1940.

Economist, The (London), *The New Deal,* Knopf, New York, 1937.

Galbraith, J. K., *American Capitalism,* Houghton Mifflin, Boston, 1956.

Galbraith, J. K., *The Affluent Society,* Houghton Mifflin, Boston, 1958.

Gilbert, Lewis D., *Dividends and Democracy,* (American Research Council) Citadel, New York, 1956.

Haynes, F. E., *Social Politics in the United States,* Houghton Mifflin, Boston, 1924.

Keynes, J. M., *The General Theory of Employment, Interest and Money,* Harcourt Brace, New York, 1936.

Knauth, Oswald, *Managerial Enterprise,* Norton, New York, 1948.

Laski, Harold J., *Grammar of Politics,* Yale University Press, New Haven, 1925.

Lasswell, Harold D., Merriam, Charles E., and Smith, T. V., *A Study of Power,* Free Press, New York, 1940.

Link, A. S., *Woodrow Wilson and the Progressive Era,* Harper and Bros., New York, 1954.

Mason, E. S., (editor) *The Corporation in Modern Society,* Harvard University Press, Cambridge, 1960.

Mills, C. W., *The Power Elite,* Oxford University Press, New York, 1959.

Myrdal, Gunnar, *An American Dilemma,* Harper and Bros., New York, 1944.

Normano, J. F., *The Spirit of American Economics,* John Day, New York, 1943.

Ogburn, William, *Social Change,* Viking, New York, 1922.

Raymond, Daniel, *The Elements of Political Economy,* 2nd ed., Kelley, New York, 1823.

Russell, Bertrand, *Power,* Norton, New York, 1938.

Smith, Adam, *The Wealth of Nations,* Modern Library, New York, 1937.

Spiegel, H. W., *The Rise of American Economic Thought,* Chilton, New York, 1960.

Ware, Caroline F. and Means, Gardiner, *The Modern Economy in Action,* Harcourt Brace, New York, 1936.

Whyte, W. H., Jr., *The Organizational Man*, Simon and Schuster, New York, 1956.

Wilcox, Clair, *Public Policies toward Business*, R. D. Irwin, Chicago, 1955.

Wilson, Woodrow, *The New Freedom*, Doubleday, Garden City, 1913.

Withers, William, *Financing Economic Security*, Columbia University Press, New York, 1939.

Wooton, Barbara, *Plan or No Plan*, Farrar and Rinehart, New York, 1935.

Wooton, Barbara, *Freedom Under Planning*, University of North Carolina Press, Chapel Hill, North Carolina, 1945.

Worthy, J. C., *Big Business and Free Men*, Harper and Bros., New York, 1959.

Index